MYWATER

The Carp Fishing Years

Elliott Symak

First published in 1989 by
Angling Publications
1 Grosvenor Square
Sheffield S2 4MS

British Library Cataloguing in Publication Data

Symak, Elliott
Mywater
1. Carp. Angling
I. Title
799.1'752

ISBN 1 871700 03 5

Produced, designed and typeset by
Angling Publications
Sheffield

Colour origination by
Colorplan, Leeds

Printed by
Joseph Ward and Son
Dewsbury

THIS BOOK IS DEDICATED TO

Mim, Jay, Boysie, Charlene, Leon and Oakley, without whom my life would not be a life at all.

Jim Gregory, B.Sc. ace perch catcher and dotter of i's.

To carp fishers everywhere – and Chris Yates in particular for writing the best book and having an irreproachable attitude.

And finally to Pooch, the sufferer for so many long years. But you won in the end, didn't you?

Love and peace, everybody

ACKNOWLEDGEMENTS

Thanks to Jim Gregory for being schoolteacher, Pooch for being a good secretary and Pooch's brother, Phil Banks, for the covers and the other pretties.

MYWATER

The Carp Fishing Years

Well, I caught a few carp and had a lot of fun and a little bit of love and never gave a snot about the numbers game and all the while the earth turned and the wind blew and I found a kind of happiness in my little, intimate game with those carp of Mywater.

Suddenly a thousand star-spangled nights had passed and I was still there and I found I had fallen in love with a woman of water, and grass and birds and green.

She had her moods, this woman. I suffered her spiteful tantrums when the squalls of skin-pricking rain were thrown at me; cold she was, at times aloof, icy patches around the margins evaporating my confidence, but, come the spring, her features softened and she ripened once again, thrusting, eager. Puberty re-born.

There has been no betrayal by my woman though; the lovers she has taken over the years being but passing fancies. Always, I know, I have remained her only true love. And so it will continue I suspect.

Now, late summer is nigh and as the sun blushes my woman's cheeks with its rays, I wander along the banks, inspecting the trees and bushes I have planted over the years. Soon I will sow more seed in my love and we will nourish our offspring together.

Preface

Had this book been published within a reasonable time period of it being written, this preface would have been unnecessary. As it happens, almost a decade has elapsed between finishing the work and its first print, so a few notes might not go amiss.

This is a book of a period in the seventies (nineteen, not Fahrenheit, although some of the time it was), covering seven years and concerning one bloke (me) and one lake (Mywater). I wrote the book in '80/81, persuaded my good and learned friend, Jim Gregory to help me tidy it up, then sent it to a couple of publishers. Having been duly rejected, the manuscript was put on a shelf, more or less until '88 when Colin McNeil, who at that time was a partner in Angling Publications, asked to read it. He must have been impressed 'cos here it is!

Everything therefore, from the introduction onwards, was written before '82. I make this point because one or two of the notions in this book are similar enough in context to those in a couple of other books published this decade, to smack of plagiarism.

Carp fishing in the seventies, eh? Interesting; much less complicated than it is nowadays. Mind you, fishing can be as complicated as anyone wants to make it. As you will see, I tend to aim for the simple life in carp fishing, just like the chap who, in my humble opinion, wrote the best fishing book ever, Chris Yates. The seventies though was a time of revolution and innovation in the carp world, especially in the latter half of the decade.

So the years went by and I read the book again. Did I smoke? Not anymore; not for eight years and now I shudder at the thought. Did we wear our hair so long in the mid seventies? How silly! Did I spend all that time fishing? Surely not. Mind you, although I spend less time fishing than I used to, my love of the sport continues to flourish.

Because I did not want the water concerned identified (Cambridgeshire is a small place!), there are one or two deliberate omissions regarding the environment surrounding Mywater including its true name. However, in 1986, my buddy Gary Spencer and I were able to buy the lake, so my little Redmire is now totally under my control and safe from the wallets of any devious persons who might happen along! It **is** a Redmire to me; always has been, even though there are no really monstrous carp in its depths. It is a lovely place; there is a quality about the water which is not found in too many fishing spots and I know my anglers enjoy their hours on its grassy banks, whether they catch carp or not.

One day I will write a book about my syndicate and the development of the water, following its purchase, but, for the moment, read on and enjoy.

Elliott Symak,
1989

Introduction

Mywater, the venue of this book, is an abandoned clay-pit of some 2 acres in size. The head of fish is quite large and, for the most part, hardly likely to inspire even the most modest 'pleasure fisherman', due to their small average size. The original carp stocks are easily traced as they were introduced during the early sixties by friends of mine. Fish up to 20 pounds were released into the lake, mainly of the mirror and leather variety, although the odd common carp was put in. Twenty years later, I am sure that most of these original fish have gone to the big carp pool in the sky, but their youngsters continue to thrive, offering good sport to the anglers clever or lucky enough to hook them.

My interest in the water developed in the sixties when I was bitten by the carp fishing bug. I caught my very first still-water carp, a common of 9¼ lb., from Mywater and had a few more to eighteen pounds or so, in the next few seasons. After 1969 I did not fish the water for several years and various reasons.

When I did return to the water, it soon became obvious that the carp fishing was interesting, varied, often demanding and, if success was reasonably good, could make an interesting story. The promise to write a book of my fishing at the lake, I first made to myself four years before actually putting pen to paper. Here is the book, detailing seven years' carp fishing and offering some of my thoughts on what myself and hundreds of other anglers do, year in, year out.

Carp fishing is something of an institution: some would say we carp fishers should be **in** an institution – and I agree! We are, though, one big family and enjoy our funny way of life, so blow those who think we are nuts. I am quick to make the point that we are not necessarily one big **happy** family, because there is quite a lot of torment in the carp fishing world, unfortunately. I am happy enough though, a fact which might come through in this book as irreverence to those who think the whole matter should be treated with great seriousness: apologies before we start then.

I am not one of those keyed-up chaps who can crouch for hours on end by the side of a set of rods and strike the split-second the visual indicator looks like it might be drawing a breath – far from it! Worlds from it! For a start, my reactions, if not ponderous, are something less than speed of light and apart from that, I tend not to enjoy sitting on my strained nerves all the time; not at Mywater, anyway.

Don't tell anyone, but my ideal, in fact, is relaxing in my bedchair, wearing only shorts, under a blazing sun, a tin of Coke in hand, a science fiction novel on my lap and a good fish sacked in the next swim along. I can get intense, and do, but basically I try to enjoy just being **alive** and sometimes that means being a lazy and inefficient slob. Sorry you whizz kids, but there we are.

If the reader yearns to read of hundreds of doubles (carp over ten pounds in weight), or lashings of twenties (carp over twenty pounds in weight), he will be disappointed. There are numbers of fish in both categories, I am pleased to say, but the character of Mywater and my inefficiency has seen to it that although the fishing was great fun, the number of carp landed could never approach the figures which are now being attained by some anglers in various parts of the country.

This is not a book of instruction on how to catch carp; the reader will no doubt soon learn how **not** to set about the job! I have deliberately tried to leave much of the debate on techniques and tackle from the text. Who cares? Primarily I want the reader to enjoy with me the thrills and spills of Mywater, not worry about where the leger stop should be placed, or what size hook should be used.

From when the events in this book begin, to the modern day, terminology has changed. A prime example is the term 'floater', now used to describe what we once used to call crust. Floater is, basically, a refined version of crust. Any change in terminology, therefore, is (although not done to a great degree), something which could hardly be avoided in a book spanning seven years.

Photographically, many of my pictures were not of good enough quality to warrant printing, never mind including in this book, and some that are included, shouldn't be scrutinised too closely! David Bailey need have no fears for his job. One trouble with us carp anglers is that we often carry around a battered, cheap camera and expect it to perform photographic miracles all the time.

I have never asked Mr. Carp what he thinks of me pricking his lip with a length of bent and sharpened high-carbon steel. I expect his opinion of me is rather low. You eat the food I show you though, don't you, Mr. Carp? I don't suppose I would be very pleased if every time my wife presented me with dinner there was the chance of rusty nails being hidden in the roast potatoes. (Come to think of it, I **have** been suffering stomach pains of late).

On the harder fished waters I should say carp lose their weight gain with worrying about being hooked! Not surprisingly, with the bait culture at its current level of sophistication, only carp suffering from anorexia nervosa stand much chance of escaping the angler's net.

I do not think we do them much harm; any carp hooked and landed are looked after and carefully returned to the water by the vast majority of carp anglers. At Mywater, substitute vast majority, with all syndicate members, and it is plain to see why the fish are in fine condition.

Finally, to end this diatribe, I must apologise in advance, to any of the Mywater syndicate members, past and present, who are miffed that their catches are not comprehensively documented herein. Unless I happened to make a note in the diaries I have kept faithfully for many years on my fishing, and from whence all the facts and figures of this book are garnered, I am afraid others' catches are not recorded. In any event, had I attempted to write up all the fish caught, I would have needed the patience of a saint, which I most certainly have not got. So you are stuck, more or less, with the choice of me – or nothing! Without attempting to be too profound, I have tried to honestly portray what I feel about being alive, about being a carp fisher, about the events I have experienced, so a lot of my heart, and some of my soul, lies bound between the covers of this book.

To the psychoanalysts who might choose to analyse me, I say: "Please keep your findings to yourself, as you might cause me some vast embarrassment."

Throughout this book, I have kept to the chronological order of events, as much as possible, but, to begin the main section, the tale of a good fish landed.

CHAPTER 1

Mosquito Jungle

I had noted a likely-looking spot in the north-west corner of the lake, near the big willow and having spotted a large carp in the unfishable swim, I was prompted to pull out a lot of the debris, hoping that whilst I was making it possible to extract a fish, I was not, in the meantime, destroying it as a spot the carp would feel safe in.

Late in the afternoon of the 21st June, I moved some of my tackle round to this swim. Observations had shown the carp liked to go into the corner, even if they did not often venture past the fringe of reeds into the little swim itself. Odd baits I had dropped in during the later weeks of the close-season had been taken – I judged by the carp, being an optimist!

The bank area of that swim – and I use the word swim loosely – consisted of dead branches, half-expired blackberry creepers and stinging nettles, all of which I had belaboured in the close-season to make a reasonably flat area from which to fish. I had left cover, of a sort, between water and bank but it still seemed to me that one good blink of my eyelids might well scare off any carp that chanced by.

In this part of the lake, when the south-westerlies blow, scum, leaves, dead insects, dust and all manner of organic and inorganic materials drift into the corner, against the reeds, forming layer after layer on the surface like the rings of a tree. Scum lanes, Rod Hutchinson describes this occurrence and for the life of me I can't think of a better description.

It was 6.45 p.m. when I crept into position with my rods and straight away I spotted a fat carp toddling through the reeds to the right. The main lake lay to the left. I baited a hook with a piece of dog meat and when the carp was out of sight, I lowered the bait onto a plate-sized patch of gravel in the centre of the swim. When the carp came back, it ignored the meat and wandered elsewhere, letting in two other fish, one of which lay to my left and looked to be over twenty pounds.

I had decided that this swim warranted the approach, if a carp took the bait, of hooking on a light clutch and allowing the fish to bolt into open water, rather than trying to play it under the rod tip. I was tackled up with 11 lbs. Platil Strong and a No. 6 hook.

The fish to the left nosed its way into the weeds, so I reeled in the rod, flicked away the Chunky and moulded a small piece of paste onto the hook. After smearing the paste with Marmite, I lowered it onto the spot the big fish had just vacated. Within seconds the carp was back and moved the bait a few inches with its lips, then he was off again. I put the rod in the rests, attached an indicator and stood up again to watch events.

A few minutes passed this time before the carp came out of the weed and hit the bait with its head. I don't know how many carp I've hooked like this – being able to watch its every action – but my heart always begins to pump hard, as on this occasion. Not being able to see the bait now, I crouched by the rod and watched the line entering the water. Twice it tightened up and dropped back, then it began to tighten again and the bobbin on the line slowly started to rise. I struck and the fish was on and heading, just as I had planned, out into the open water. Boy, did that one go! Yards of line sizzled off the clutch but I kept on enough pressure to ensure it helped tire the fish, whilst not enough to stop his headlong flight. Eventually he stopped and the fight carried on from there. I knew that if I tried to get the fish back into the swim, even if he was tired, there was a good chance he would give one flip of his tail and be lost in the tangle of bramble that stooped into the water on my right, so I decided that I had better enter the water myself.

I waded in, boots and all, then found that the water was deeper than I had thought, so I had to fight my way out of my jacket and throw it on the bank before I could go any further. I finished up to my navel in the cool water, standing level with the fringe of thinned-out reeds he had gone through, with eight feet of water ready to engulf me at the next step. The line was running under a large branch floating on the surface, which I hadn't spotted previously, so I spent a while grabbing hold of it and freeing the line. Fortunately, the carp didn't do anything dangerous whilst I fiddled around. I threw the branch away but in the wrong direction, typically, right onto my drop on nylon, only this time out of reach!

The sawing action continued, and if you have never tried sawing a lump of wood in half with 11 lb. line, then I can tell you, the wood usually wins. Thankfully, however, after a seemingly long period, the line was the winner for a change and the branch finally came free, allowing me to play my carp in peace.

That fish gave a scrap and a half, out there in open water, but he never went for the reeds and I was able to pull him to the net. Twice he found more reserves of energy and shot off, on spotting the net, but the third time I was lucky and he was netted safely. I bit the line, chucked the rod onto my jacket and waded back the way I had muddily come. Jed arrived from the other side of the lake shortly after the fun and games had finished and scratched his head at the swim whilst saying complimentary things about the carp. The

I waded in, boots and all…

prize for my efforts was a 20 lb. 4 oz. mirror and that is how the Twenty Swim was named.

Jed took some photographs for me, then I organised my pitch for the night and went home to change into fresh clothing and dry out the contents of my wallet, which I had forgotten was in my back pocket. The moths in the banknote section were all drowned, unfortunately.

I arrived back at the lake at 9.00 p.m. and scrounged a cup of tea off Jed, had a chat with Nige, then settled down for the night in the hopes of another big one from the Twenty Swim; I blanked.

In the previous close-season I had been fishing another old clay pit which was to be filled with fly-ash under the C.E.G.B.'s Land Reclamation Scheme. Some time during the day, sport being non-existent, I went for a walk to the other side of the pit to see an acquaintance of mine, Ginger. During the ensuing conversation, it transpired that Mywater was under new ownership, was still a good carp fishery and was being run as a syndicate. This information led me, eventually, to the owner who, during the week before the season opened, allowed me to join the syndicate. That chance encounter with Ginger had paved the way for years of fun and games.

During my first trip, ten days after the season started, the heavens opened up and the wind became violent – so much so that I spent a while just holding onto the brolly so it wouldn't blow away and allow me to end up soaked. Not a very auspicious start.

I caught a tench, a perch, got a soaking foot and a damp backside, then spent the night catching nothing. Some time after 7.00 a.m. I had a walk round the lake, saw little worth throwing a bait at, so went into town for provisions. On arriving back at the water, I walked round again and discovered that it was just possible to fish in the (later to be named) Moped Swim. A number of carp, one looking over twenty pounds, were mooching about so I went back for a suitable rod.

The swim itself, waterside, was much as it is today, with light patches of hornwort being the main visible weed, whilst light weed covers much of the bottom. The water depth, shelving from three feet at the bank to about seven feet deep in the centre of the swim, makes seeing much of the bottom an impossibility. Norfolk reed was abundant to right and left of the opening I could fish through. Bankside was a veritable jungle of frail trees, hawthorn and blackthorn bushes, wild roses, bramble and, where a patch of ground actually managed to see the sun now and then, nettles. All these obstacles seemed to delight in grabbing, scratching, stinging and generally making life uncomfortable for anyone who dared enter their hallowed sanctuary.

Ensconced near the water's edge, I pinched a swan shot on the line a foot from the hook and cast in a piece of Hovis crust and watched it float against the reeds until the rudd had knocked it about enough for the shot to counteract the buoyancy of the bait. Slowly the bread sank into three feet of water where bank and reeds formed a four foot wide channel. Some while later, the line jerked and began to trickle out. The strike resulted in a fish and a snag, both seemingly well held! The snag proved to be a yard long branch, which sportingly fell off the line; the fish, of rather more modest proportions, had the decency to keep hanging on long enough for me to net it. An 11 lb. common.

The rest of that initial trip was not very exciting, but I did manage to get soaked through, scrounged a tow off a local farmer, as my car wouldn't start, and removed and replaced the starter motor before going damply and oilily home to all those little things a fishing session in the rain often does not provide – like a warm meal, a warm bed and a warm lady.

That first trip had produced a double with which I was well pleased, but the water itself was enough to generate a feeling of well-being in anyone who appreciates a pleasant fishing spot. It was, and still is, a good water to fish, where carp can usually be spotted, if not hooked; peace and quiet can be had most of the time and that magic quality we read about in 'Drop Me A Line', of silent carp pools, is there with just a mite of imagination. When Terry Eustace came to fish the water one night, he stood on the banks saying, in that thick Brummy accent of his, "Innit sexy." I had never quite thought of the water as being sexy – but I knew what Terry meant!

The long north side has a grass-verged lane as the boundary. The drop from lane to water is about fifteen feet, with the slope of the bank at something like 45 degrees, putting the water edge an average of fifteen feet from the lane. Tall thorn bushes, mostly set back from the water's edge, cover the south side and the west end, with blackberry bushes filling in some of the gaps. At the east end, alder trees and blackthorn fight their duels for a place to flourish on the Earth, forming a solid barrier against the elements.

The effect of the high bank and all the cover is that the worst of the weather is not felt on Mywater. Only when the wind is blowing strongly from the south or west, does it really make an impression on the lake's surface.

The eastern end of the lake finishes in a stagnant, reed filled pool from which flows an outlet further up the lake, discharging into the small pool. We blocked that off in the second year of joining the syndicate and enlarged the lower outlet. Much more logical, it seems to me, to have an outlet leave the bottom of the lake rather than via a side exit. The small pool has in it some small fish, numerous pike and a lot of dead bushes and branches.

The 'Island' of course, isn't one at all, but its nature makes it seem like one, with water both sides, so that is the name we bestowed upon that stretch of land from the very early days.

Reflecting on Mywater, the water level has risen somewhat since I had last fished it and one or two pitches were now unfishable. It was a typically neglected water.

The lake averages nine feet in depth, with the areas alongside the lane varying between three feet to, in the New Swim, ten feet. That side was an unfishable jungle for the most part when I first joined the syndicate. On the map of the lake will be seen quite large areas of reeds. In the main we have left the reedbeds alone as we have seen no pressing need to remove them. The sharp delineation of the reeds, particularly on the north side, is due to ridges of clay, 2 – 3 feet wide, which rise 6 – 7 feet from the floor of the pit. When reeds colonised the water they were able to survive on the ridges but not, of course, in the deeper water. Silting of the north side swims and one or two other areas has assisted the spreading of the reeds. I am sure the carp browse on the weed coated ridges.

The two weeks following my first trip were as much for reconnoitring as fishing, although I did manage to hook a couple of carp in the bad areas along the lane side. I managed to lose 'em as well.

I began, straight away, to pick at the outlet stream which had been dammed and by the second week in July, the water level had dropped nine inches or so. It was my intention to have more than half a dozen fishable swims by the end of the season. I might seem to have crashed into the syndicate and taken over the destruction (called improvement) of the water without so much as a by your leave, but in fact, the owner, learning of my single-mindedness, had given me a free hand to alter the environment. I would have done it anyway, unless my actions were obviously causing trouble.

On the 10th July, I braved thorn, bramble and stinging nettle, not to mention the damned mosquitoes which frequent the water in droves, to fish in a gap I had made a few days previously alongside the Swamp. I managed to

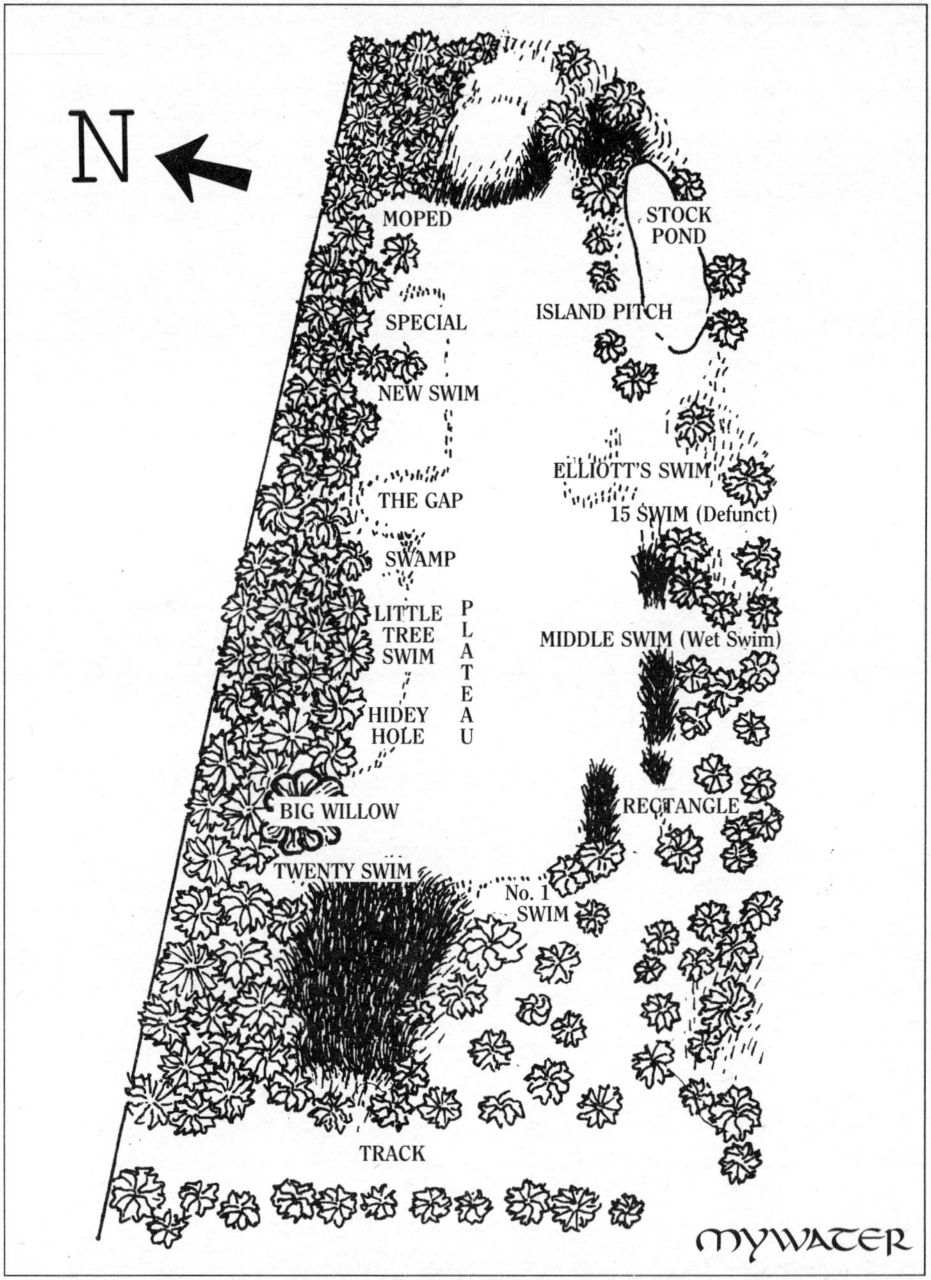

MAP ON PAGE 10

coax a couple of baits into the water, despite the attempts of the undergrowth to rip my line to shreds, and was sitting quietly, minding my own business, when one of the rods took up ballet dancing; a carp had hooked itself. The fight was a short tug of war; although the reeds and general debris I had cast into seemed intent on the carp staying where it was: 30 lbs. braided terylene and strong carp rod considered otherwise and a $14^1/_2$ lb. leather was soon in the net.

Towards the end of the month, my manipulation of the north-side undergrowth was beginning to overtake the fishing. With the help of Nigel Bryant (who had joined the syndicate at the same time as me and with whom I teamed up), I attacked the Special Swim and started into the New Swim. To end our joint venture in the Special I decided to fire the bank, as much in exasperation as anything. There wasn't much breeze coming off the water when I lit some dried grass, but the way the farrago went woosh, you would have thought a force ten was blowing napalm up the bank. Boy, did it go! By the time I had the conflagration under control I had black hands and face but the makings of a swim was there. That was how the Special became tenable.

Never one to learn a lesson quickly, I did the same stupid trick a day or two later, next door in the New Swim and this time only the gap I had made, leading down to the Swamp, saved the whole north side from going up. But at least the New Swim was now fishable. We christened it the New Swim because the Special, although nameless at the time, had been part-habitable for a short time, so the New Swim was the newest. The logic of these carp anglers never ceases to amaze!

To this day, eight years later, the New Swim has still not completely recovered from that fire, nor have the thorns along the lane behind it, there being still a thinning of the foliage over which the carp are spotted swimming in the sunken tree by any angler, dog walker or local ruffian who happens by. The grass in that spot is actually worn bare by the shuffling of countless feet.

I spent the next two fishing sessions in the Special. I see, from later notes in my log, that it was initially called Nigel's Swim, but the events beginning the 1st September changed that.

The two trips to the Special were blanks but, undeterred, I arrived at Mywater at 6.30 p.m. on the last day of August. It was a Friday and I tackled up once more in the Special, with three rods which were baited with Kit-e-Kat, sausage and a fried special of indeterminate ancestry. The fried specials were prepared in the normal way (i.e. mixed and rolled to a recipe) then cooked in the chip pan for one to four minutes, depending on the size and consistency of the ball. If the mix is right (with my cooking there is never any telling), and the baits are drained well, they will float. The ancestry of the bait in question was unknown because once fried, the colour of the baits are uniform, more or less, whatever the ingredient and broken open they do not give their secret to me. When I was born, He, in His infinite wisdom, gave me looks, talent, yes, but no sense of smell, so any baits I fry become a fried bait and that is that. This nasal organ that is only good for collecting air-borne debris before it hits my lungs is increasingly becoming a bane with me, I must confess. It is a bit of a joke amongst the people who know me, amongst the other things about me that must be a bit of a joke. I **can** smell ammonia, by the way, but I doubt if such a bait would interest carp.

I digress.

It may seem surprising that I used three different baits in an area of 45' x 20' which is about what the Special encompasses, but I rarely use the same bait on all rods unless something is obviously 'going' well and on these exploratory trips I didn't really know what bait to use. As far as groundbaiting is concerned, if I am confident the fish will appear in the swim, then I throw in a very few free offerings – perhaps half a dozen or less. This cuts down the odds of the hookbait being left, should a carp fancy a nibble or two. During the course of a sitting, if I consider the sprats are whittling away the baits, then I throw in a few more baits. It's real text book stuff this, isn't it?

The water in the Special goes to something like 8 feet deep, with the main feature of the swim, apart from the reeds, being a large sunken tree to the right of the pitch, which must have grown before the claypit was allowed to flood. A certain amount of hornwort dots the swim, with a fringe of grass-like weed growing on the slope of the swim in about 4 feet of water, and parallel with the bank. A gap through which the rods poke is the only break in the vegetation. Some immature trees make every effort to rise about the brambles, but few succeed.

At 1.45 a.m. having had a sausage special and a couple of Kit-e-Kat specials eaten off the hook, I hit a bite on 'Kat' which started as a jerk then turned into a run. The strike was at the right time, because a carp was on. At first, due to the inactiveness of the beast, I thought I had hooked a tench, but then it began to move strongly and take line. The fish was on for half a minute but then it got into the branches of the sunken tree to the right and I could only tug away at the snag until the line broke.

One more jerk of the indicator, within twenty minutes of losing the fish showed that there was still something down there, so I reeled in the fried special which had been floating on the surface near the reeds all night, pinched on a swan shot six inches from the hook and cast it out, the bait now sinking and near to the snag.

At 6.00 a.m. one of the buzzers sounded and the indicator on the fried special rod was rattling in the butt ring. I grabbed the rod, trapped the line and struck, in one action, feeling a big fish on. I don't remember knocking over the bale arm.

The fish had moved to the left and felt as if it was round a snag, only the snag was on the move with the fish, it seemed. Something rolled on the far side of the reeds, to the left and it dawned on me that the fish had gone through those reeds on taking the bait. I eventually pumped the fish back through the reeds and it shot towards me, then performed a sharp left turn and went between the sunken tree and the bank – a gap of about 2 feet.

I had on heavy line so I was, thankfully, able to pull the fish back in front of me, but it then did the same trick again. I kept the rod high, fingers on the clutch so no line could be taken and almost pulled its head out of the water to turn it from that danger area. Fortunately, the ploy worked, and after a scary second's floundering against that tough old tree, the fish was in front of me once again and netted in short order.

I shouted Nige, who was fishing the bottom swim (No. 1) that the fish was about eighteen pounds and to come round to take some photographs. I struggled up the bank with the fish and was a bit weak kneed by the time Nige arrived. He estimated the fish to be over twenty and read the scales whilst I lifted them. It was 23 lbs. in weight, a lovely mirror and my first stillwater twenty.

We were both due at work that morning so the photo session was enacted straight away. The shots were taken at a 30th sec., with the lens aperture set at f2.8 because of the weak light. Somehow those pictures came out fairly well, despite being taken on just about the worst settings you can impose on the film. My resources didn't run to a flash gun in those days.

After my four hour stint at work, I was back at the water for 1.00 p.m., my tackle still in the Special. The day, like the previous one, was a windy devil, which made bite-indication difficult to say the least.

It had filtered through my woollen brain that the carp were so keen on the baits and so confident in the swim that they were eating their food on the

A nice double figure leather (top) and an $18^{1}/_{2}$lbs of mirror. Lovely!

spot and spitting out the hook most of the time, so I was ready for hitting twitches, or at least as ready as I ever would be. Somehow though, being of a dilatory nature, I am afraid I never hit any twitches at all. I blanked during the night but at 6.00 a.m. on the Sunday morning, a fish was hooked which went straight into the tree and snagged the line, which didn't break, for a change. I could feel the fish still on as I tried to fee the line but nothing wanted to give, so I cursed my luck and decided to go in after the quarry.

The rod in the rests, with the line tight, I stripped off in that cold dawn, with some foreboding. The water was a sight colder to my naked flesh than the air and I wondered, by the time it reached my navel, whether it was worth it at all. By the time I was up to my neck, straddling the branches of the tree like a white, aquatic monkey, I regained what bit of sanity I had and decided that I was only going to achieve, perhaps, waterlogged lungs, so I struggled back to terra firma and dried off as best I could. The fish, in the meantime, had broken free and I reeled in a hookless line.

It wasn't until 4.00 a.m. the next morning that I hit another carp, on a four inch lift of the indicator, which tried its damnedest to go through the tree. Even I can play 'em right some of the time and this was one of those times, with me showing old cypry just who the boss was, until the fish eventually gave up the fight and was netted. 18$^1/_2$ lbs. of mirror that one was. Lovely!

In the afternoon, I had about four baits eaten off the hooks. The wind, a south westerly, was so bad that I had a task deciding which line movements were fish and which were the action of the wind. With the opportunities missed, no carp were hooked. Casting out after having missed a 'take', I was setting the rod in the rest when it jerked in my hands with a taking carp, so that one had to be rebaited. Trying a float later on in an attempt to hit a 'lift' bite I had the float go down instead of rising up and was so surprised that the float was rising again before I struck – at nothing! Later on, another bobbin jerked and this time, despite striking at nothing, the hook had gone. "So you're making weapons down there now, are you?" I thought to myself.

In retrospect, the day could have been handled differently and I could have had one or two carp on the bank as they were obviously devouring the baits with gusto, but retrospective thinking only comes after the event – when it is too late. One of the continuing drawbacks with the Special Swim is that the rods have to be placed to the left of the angler – a situation which does not suit me at all, despite being left handed.

Dusk-time double.

I did manage to successfully hit one of those perfunctory bites, at 4.30 the next morning, and landed the fish too, which was a common of 15 lbs. After all the attention the specials had received over this period, the swim just had to be christened the Special and thus it was.

I fished some more that month, with no carp to show for it, did a lot of watching of carp in the various areas they frequented and continued knocking the bankside clutter about. Nige, managing to fish the Special Swim after I had had my fling, landed a mirror of 17 lbs. – again to 'Kat'.

* * *

Baked beans, burnt boiled; luncheon meat cubes shared with the carp, fried in the pan with greasy eggs. Butter always too hard at dawn, too soft at dusk, smeared on ragged hunks of bread. Too many cigars, the tar bitter, sliced off the mouth end with a razor blade. Tiredness, aches, pains. Opening tins of spaghetti with anything sharp that will do the job because the can-opener is in the kitchen drawer back home. Cups of welcome tea with globules of dried milk floating undissolved and indissoluble on the oily surface. Flies in the tea – gnats with a death-wish riding the film as corpses. Extra meat, I suppose. Ugh!

* * *

I lost more than one carp from the Special Swim over the next fortnight – all but one getting into the tree and severing the line. I should really have abandoned the pitch until such time as I was capable of fishing it efficiently.

I cleared out the Moped swim during this period, also the Hidey Hole, the Swamp and the Little Tree Swim.

The Hidey Hole was soon endowed with a name because it was so hidden from view that for a while, only Nige and I knew about it! The Little Tree was so named because sited alongside the channel of water it comprises, was a little tree – well, several actually, but we could hardly call it the Several Little Trees Swim, could we? This swim has never been one for comfortable fishing, night or day, but the passage of the carp between the Swamp and the Hidey Hole make for interesting viewing in the Little Tree area. The shallowness of the water here – 3 feet – is probably the main reason why the carp are rarely hooked. The Swamp was, and still is, a swamp; a shallow area of weed and reed and broken branches which was impossible to fish, initially, and still requires attention every year to keep the reeds at a manageable level.

13th of March double from the Special Swim.

Mucky, messy March time in the Special Swim.

During the early days, it seemed that Nige and I were the two syndicate members most interested in the water in general, rather than in just its inhabitants. That is not to say we fished it the most, but it was N. B. and myself who became involved with the place, so it fell to us to find all the names for the pitches. As I tended to do a little more work, I collared the biggest say, so a bit more of **me** went into Mywater as time progressed. The need for names of pitches wasn't particularly discussed, they just came naturally, as an incident occurred, or a set of circumstances pointed in a certain direction. On a lake such as Mywater, with no two swims being alike, there was never any confusion as the names were dreamed up and integrated into the conversations we had about the water.

Nige and I visited the water quite frequently during the winter but we didn't fish it exclusively for carp. Primarily, our trips were to catch live-bait, with a couple of carp rods cast out just in case Cypry felt peckish. This way of carrying on isn't exactly conducive to good carp fishing and, needless to say, we didn't catch many carp, only one in fact, of 13 lbs., to Nige.

My last double of the season, on a proper carp fishing trip, came at 9.40 p.m. on the 13th March. Having a rare night trip to the water, I had plumped for the Special (surprise, surprise) and managed to land a slim common of 15½ lbs. on a summer-sized 'Kat' special.

It is obvious from what happened during the previous September, that I wasn't as sharp at hauling the carp from the main swim as I would have liked to be. The tree in the Special cost me a great deal of heartache but had it not been there, then nor would the carp with such frequency. I had not learnt, at that time, that it is possible to hold a fish without it gaining an inch of line from the reel, provided the hook-hold is good and the line and hook are up to standard. A soft rod helps too.

The trouble with that swim in particular, of course, was that the devils were often in the tree before a bite registered. Later on I removed a small number of the worst branches, or cut them back at least, so the losses in future seasons were reduced.

* * *

CHAPTER 2

The Hidey Hole

By 7.30pm on the 15th I was settled down, with the rods waiting in their rests to be baited. Settled down in the Special, I might add. I claimed that for the start during the close season. Two of the syndicate members were on the far bank, set for the week.

Nige came down shortly after 8pm and shoved me out of the way so he could carry his gear into the New swim, accessible only via the Special. As he set up I watched carp drift around on the surface; nothing very big, but I wasn't too worried about sizes; what swims about on the top of an eight feet deep swim often has no bearing on what is on the bottom where the baits are going to be. As surface baits had been proved to be a waste of time, generally, my concoctions were mainly boiled specials.

It was a warm evening, with little wind and I threw in a few of the 'Kat baits, watching the ripples lap against the branches of the tree that had caused a lot of my problems the year before. The carp, by now, had gone. Ginger came down at 9.30 and elected to fish in the Little Tree Swim – probably the most awkward place to spend the night. By 10 o'clock we could stand the strain of waiting no longer and by mutual agreement Nige and I cast into our respective bits of the pond.

The number of small fry in the lake never seems to diminish and their taste for our baits tends to increase the more we throw in. Thus we both suffered twitches and butt-ringers for ages, none of which we could hit. Nige had even more bother than myself but I reckon that the roach, rudd and bream were attracted by all the carbon that had found its way into that swim after my fires the previous summer!

Round about 12.15 my swim went dead and only a couple of bleeps from the antennas startled me until shortly after 1am when the bobbin on the rod cast next to the sunken tree began moving pretty fast up to the butt ring. In the close season the Special had been re-arranged a little so that it was now possible to have the bed-chair right next to the rods, consequently I was in a better position for action and the quicker strike met with solid resistance. Initially, with that tremendous surge a big carp can produce when feeling the hook, a small amount of line was taken off the spool, but I had set the reel clutches tight before dark so it was going to have to be a big fish to even budge them. I soon knew it **was** a big fish by the way it moved slowly but surely round the swim, giving, every now and then, a heavy tug just to let me know I had a job on my hands.

Nige was behind me within half a minute and I told him several times

"You stayed awake for your dream, mate."   Early season eye-opener! 25lb 8oz from The Special.

that I was into a big 'un, whilst I strained to stop the fish boring into the tree and, perhaps, freedom. Eventually, after I had put my finger onto the spool for the last time, he seemed ready for the net.

There was only enough room in the gap I had been fishing through for one man, so I had to net the fish myself. It was pitch-black, the carp was difficult to see and the first netting attempt produced water only! The second time I brought the carp in the right position, more by luck than judgement and a steady lift put me in the right position to say, "He's mine."

Ginger had appeared on the scene by then and he helped me to carry the fish up the bank and on to the grass verge by the lane. Both he and Nige thought the fish was a twenty and were proved right when the scales went down to 25lbs. 8oz. And the season only one and a half hours young! So later on I said jokingly to Nige, "I didn't even get chance for a wink of sleep tonight," to which he answered: "You stayed awake for your dream, mate."

The bait had been a large ball of Kit-e-Kat, meal and flour mixed with eggs and boiled for a couple of minutes. The rod was a split cane 2 lbs. test curve rod. The line, which I'd been using for over a decade (not the same bit) in snaggy swims, was braided terylene and the hook a 1.0 Goldstrike with the point stoned down to form just a blob with the stoned down barb. I know modern thinking dictates a long, needle-like hook point **but,** the inevitable violence which occurs when you hook a carp on only fifteen feet of line, and the nose of that fish next to a dirty great snag, brings into question the vulnerability of a needle point in that split second of the strike. Should the point connect with the tough part of the carp's mouth it could either bend over at the point and drag out, or break off at the barb. Both have happened to me. Many writers say they slowly and firmly pull into a fish when the bite registers; for myself, when a submerged tree is the carp's quick route to escape, I give a fast and strong yank and hold on. So I've put back carp fishing ten years. Mind you, the higher-carbon wire hooks can give a better reliance than some of the rubbish we have had to put up with.

* * *

Spare a thought for the guys who didn't catch a carp on June 16th. Give consideration to their shattered hopes, the hapless plans – washed away in a steam of unimpassioned sloth by the quarry. Smiles of joy are outnumbered by the many tears of anguish. The carp are the winners by far: the carp become fat on the close-season feeds, then sink into deeper

water as the noisy footsteps descend the bank; as the rests grate down through the gravel, taking a rigid and vertical stance for all the world and all the carp to see.

* * *

Feeling cock o' the north, or, more accurately, East Anglia, I had my picture taken with my catch when the morning light was strong enough and slipped him back to give contest another day. The following night was very quiet – I don't think I struck at all. After the Lord Mayor's Show…

The syndicate members were all using 'Kat' at the start of that season and it produced a couple of fish: a few days after the start I called in at Mywater en-route to another lake and saw a member on the far bank landing a nineteen pounder. He had earlier caught a fish of $13^1/_2$lbs.

The carp began spawning that night, around the fibrous roots of the big willow. During the morning I sat in the tree and watched the fish gliding and thrashing in pairs, quartets – any combination – performing the fascinating ritual which would decide the future stocks of the lake.

When the wind is able to ruffle the surface of Mywater, the carp love to follow it. Such was the situation I found a few days later when, the spawning cycle having run its course, I went to try my luck.

The wind was blowing into No. 1 Swim so I chose to sit in the fork of the big tree. The big tree, an old, gnarled willow, is almost two trees. The thick main trunk grows straight out from the bank, whilst the minor trunk veers to the right, rising only slightly from the horizontal until it ends, six feet above the water, almost over the Twenty Swim. At some period of the tree's life the sheer weight of it loosened the roots' hold on the crumbly bank and the tree fell over into the water. After the period during which the tree recovered from its trauma, it grew upwards again, reaching for the sun. The consequence of this accident of nature is that the first twenty five feet of the thick trunk is horizontal and just above water level, making a convenient causeway for us to get past the clinging bankside growth. The water here is weeded and reeded – not until the trunk heads in a more vertical direction does the water below it reach a depth worthy of more than cursory interest from the carp, where the fibrous roots and fallen branches form a jungle which the small fish always and the carp sometimes tenant.

As a spotting tree the willow is excellent, allowing the whole of the west end of the lake to be viewed. Many an hour have I spent up there, watching the surface fish wander around with all the time in the world to explore their home.

The base of the trunk, above the deeper water, has several branches growing from it, some of which I had sawn off in the close season and one of which I sat on, with a crusting rod balanced on my knees, a float rod offering live shrimps and requiring some dexterity to use. Fishing the shrimps below the rod tip merely occasioned the interest of small roach and the Billy Bunters of the small fish world – perch. The crust rod produced a carp. Nige netted it for me and it went 15lbs., a dark, slim common which battled all the way to the net. Hours later I caught the $20^1/_4$lb. fish which features in the initial tale of this book.

* * *

I lie unmoving, the rousing world moving instead around me. The breeze shakes russet leaves, breaking their dead grip on the twig. Clouds ride the wind, high up, no portent of rain, only the reminder that, should they incline downwards, I may be compelled to move and hide under my canvas.

Body aches: silent testimony of too many hours reclining on an aluminium and cotton bed. Eyes sting with sleep, bladder presses for relief.

The early morning bee alights delicately on a dew-covered petal, searching for the nectar of summer to carry back to its hive. A squirrel, with a grasp and a wrench of furry hand shows no such daintiness when taking the berry from the tree.

Dead grass and weed lay muddily tangled, trampled; a rectangular outline will be revealed when I break camp, with two indented lines where the bed-chair has taken my weight and tried to escape from it into the earth. Creak of bones as I re-position my sore buttocks and a black, enigmatic spider scurries from a crease in the blanket and rides the waves of the cloth like a camel travelling the desert dunes.

* * *

The fishing sessions I enjoyed during the next few weeks at Mywater were non-productive from a carp caught point of view. Only odd bream fell to

"Say cheese" for a common.

my baits, but it was, nonetheless, all good, clean, fun. During one session, fishing No. 1 swim (so named because it is the first swim you come across if entering the property through the five-barred gate by the lane) I survived the most tremendous thunderstorm.

Having second sight, Nige had gone home shortly before the heavens opened up their box of tricks but I decided to stay a while longer, as the weather seemed 'right'.

A drop of warm rain landed on my cheek and trickled down like a precious tear. Another alighted in my eye as I looked upwards, a knife thrust sharply. The black clouds to the east were pushing their lighter brethren over my head and I knew that soon I would be besieged. And so I was, the wind increasing in strength until it howled, blowing my umbrella inside out: I sat grimly hanging on whilst Mother Nature threw her arms around me, trying to squeeze the breath from my lungs and blow in her rain. The rain lashed the water surface like a blanket of frenziedly wriggling demons as the thunder and lightning suddenly upon me gave a savage display, as if challenging puny man to a duel.

Whilst holding the bounding umbrella against the elements I knew that if a carp were indiscreet enough to run off with a bait I sure as hell wasn't going to get out from under and strike.

Good fortune shone on me amidst the chaos, though: I wasn't reduced to ash by lightning hitting the brolly pole, nor did a fish touch my baits.

One thing I love, when the weather is hot and I am not likely to upset anyone, is to strip off and enter the water for a cooling swim. In the back of my mind there is always the thought that a pike might attack my extremities, but that is a small risk to take. During the period following the twenty I swam several times and thus the Plateau came to light. We knew that this part of the lake was shallow (about 5-6 feet deep instead of the usual 8-9 feet) but it was not until my investigatory swim that we realised just how extensive the area really was. On it was a layer of coarse, short weed different in nature to the other weeds in the water except the stuff which adorned the slopes of the 'ridges. The Plateau has since produced quite a number of carp.

The patch of reeds directly to the left of the Mud Swim had, years before, been fishable and as we had now lowered the water level by about a foot it seemed a good idea to test the reedy promontory. I was pleased to find that, at the risk of wet feet, I could fish it.

This pitch gave better access to the Gap, with a directly forward cast reaching the haven the carp seemed to like. Although it later became Elliott's Swim, due to work I did on it, at that time I merely made it temporarily habitable. To save any confusion, I will refer to this swim as 'Elliott's Swim', although to me, of course, it is 'my swim'.

My swimming also revealed that the trout pellet baits that Nige and I had been putting into the water were all going in short order, but we certainly were not catching any fish on them. Apart, that is, from a solitary bream – to Nige!

The Special Swim, so much in the limelight that past season and the beginning of the current one was now not worth bothering with. Much of the time there was an angler braving the sunken tree, but nothing was turning up. Blanks were the order of the day – and the night.

It was not until August 10th, a Saturday, that I managed to catch another double. Taken off Elliott's Swim, the capture shows that thoughtful fishing isn't always the way to success.

At that time I was into legering baits cast more than a few yards - in this case on to the Plateau and with the hook end 'bombed up'. I had spent up until 1.30 a.m. catching only a $1^1/_2$lbs. bream. That fish resulted in the lead on the line tangling with something and eventually breaking off the short length of light nylon it was tied to. As I couldn't be bothered to put on another lead, I cast out the ball of bait a few yards, into nine feet of water, just in front of me. At dawn, I had on this rod one of the classic runs we often got at Mywater, which duly resulted in the fight far less spectacular than the run and a common of $15^1/_4$lbs. was the result. I thought to myself, returning the fish to the water, 'It just goes to show that perhaps we will catch more if we close our minds and eyes and fish like fools'. We had, in fact, been trying out small paste baits or bits of specials in the hopes of catching the carp with greater ease. That fish taking a bait over an inch in diameter, confounded the issue somewhat.

* * *

Well the fishing's off, the money's no good but still I keep going. Wonder why? Fortunately, it isn't necessary to tramp miles over ploughed fields to transport the tackle; thank the Gods the walk is short. Be nice to hook a carp, even if I lost it in the reeds – at least there would be a bit of excitement. At least the adrenalin would pump through the heart at a good rate. Well, nothing for it but to count the reeds across the way – I wonder

how long that will take. Probably the moorhens have already done that, they sit in 'em all the time. Anyone would think we persecute them, which we don't. Wouldn't even mind hooking a moorhen, come to think of it; be nice to see the rod bent on something other than a weedbed or those ever present reeds. Mywater must have more reeds per carp than any water I know. Than any water known to man, I reckon, 'cos the carp must all be dead.To be philosophical, though, there is always tomorrow.

* * *

When I am fishing, or just visiting the lake, I usually put in a few of the baits I fancy using in the future; $^3/_8$" cubes of luncheon meat and broad beans were two such baits. As well as these I was still putting in trout pellet paste in the hopes that it would one day work. This bait planting is a habit I have slipped into over the years which can actually be self-defeating, as the sprats soon acquire a taste for new offerings and thus make themselves a pain in the neck. Rightly or wrongly, though, I still do my planting and there must be many baits that the carp have eaten but which I have never given a proper trial.

The Hidey Hole

Towards the middle of August, my interest was directed to the Hidey Hole. The swim is merely a continuation of the Swamp and Little Tree Swims. It is around 15 feet between the bank and the reed fringe, over or through which the lines are cast onto the Plateau. The long channel from the Swamp terminates to the right of the Hidey Hole in a patch of reeds. To the left is a large bush which overhangs the water. The bottom of the swim consists of patches of light weed growing on silt, which is at least two feet deep in places, with three feet of water above this. The area is oft' visited by the carp, who love to sun themselves on the surface, surrounded by cover. As is usually the case with the northside shallow areas, the carp rarely get their heads down for a good old stir. In fact, there seems to be an uncanny ability on the part of the carp, to detect an angler on the bank in the Hidey Hole or Little Tree. Probably because of their canniness, I have not been able to catch a carp actually in the patch of water which is the Hidey Hole Swim, hence the casts onto the Plateau – which, fortunately for the angler, is favoured by the carp.

My first success in the Hidey Hole came on the 26th August; I had battered the swim, in the preceding few weeks, more or less to my liking on the bank. In the water, during my swims, I had uprooted the reeds on the clay ridge to enlarge the previously small gap. Now I felt confident that the swim was worth the hassle of getting all the paraphernalia needed for a couple of days' fishing down the woody slope from the lane, over the trunk of the big tree and along the thorn-avenued path to the swim.

I stopped my car on the gravel lane and turned off the headlights, sitting for a while, taking in the darkness and silence of this lonely spot. It was approaching midnight when I stepped from the motor. The reason for the lateness of the hour was my continued fight to bring some kind of normality to my household – which necessitates me being there! I try to give my wife and children, three at this time, as much of my time as possible, no doubt subconsciously trying to cancel out the guilt I feel at spending so many hours fishing. Sundays especially, I try to be at home – certainly Saturday night fishing is out, except on very rare occasions.

When the mind and body is tired and a warm house and family silently insist that dad would be better off where he is, it is hard to put one foot in front of the other – in the direction of the back door; but, innumerable times I have headed for that door, inexplicably under a cloud of depression which often besets me just before going fishing. Of course, you can't catch 'em if you are sitting watching T.V., so out of the door it is. The effort was particularly hard that night as it had been raining for much of the day, and still was, as I loaded up the car. Nonetheless, I tried to ignore the elements and carried on with the job. A final check found me satisfied and on my way, my depression lifting as I neared the water.

The rain must have been in a good mood because it petered out as I reached my destination and held off long enough for me to slip and trip into the Hidey Hole. I failed to be quiet, in the pitch darkness, but hoped my clumsy feet would not scare the carp too much. Two rods were used, one on 'Kat', the other baited with broad bean and both were cast onto the Plateau. I had a 'Kat' taken off the hook in the night, but missed that bite. The rain had begun again and continued, unabated, until a short time before dawn.

I woke at 6.00 a. m. gummy-eyed. The indicators, silver paper cylinders, were up near the butt rings of the rods, suggesting the lines had been pulled, if only gently, during the dark hours. Shivering in the morning chill, I lit a smoke, coughed a little and tried a mouthful of muddy liquid from the flask, which had stood sentry-stiff by my side all night. One mouthful was enough to show me I needed to boil the kettle. I spat out the tepid tea and groaned inwardly, not wanting the bother of brewing up but desiring something hot to wash away the night tastes in my mouth. I lay back a little while longer, the bleep of the buzzer making me jump once, then, with an effort, I rolled away the groundsheet and blankets, put my feet on the muddy ground and stood slowly up. A moorhen in the nearby reeds, startled by my intrusion into its morning routine, took off with a squawk and a clatter on a surface-kissing flight to the far bank. My heart, given a jolt by the sudden breaking of the quiet, pounded inside my chest.

The kettle was soon atop the blue flames of the stove and I slapped a little fresh water onto my face before going to the side of the swim to answer nature's call. Barely had I finished my chore before the buzzer emitted its rasping call. The noise stopped as I reached the rods and I gave a mental shrug, debating whether to re-bait or drink tea. The decision was taken from my hands by a further noise from the buzzer and more movements of an indicator. I picked up the offending rod and found that the line was round the reeds but not snagged. I reeled in a dead weight and found attached a 12½lb. common! The 'Kat' bait I had re-cast in the night had gone but that, I kidded myself, was more likely down the gullets of the rapacious sprat which could beat all but the hardest specials to death.

Having become wet during the night and morning, I went home to dry out and was back about 4.00 p.m., settling down again in the Hidey Hole, where I suffered a fruitless night. During the day, the broad bean baits were jiggled about unmercifully, with any strikes I made just a waste of time. One bite, which was almost certainly given by a carp, jerked up the bobbins and pulled round the rod top, but I was too late getting to it. Damn. I had been fishing with the bale-arm open all day in the hopes of a run, but had decided, shortly before, to fish bale-arm closed, but that bite was too fast. Why I did not get to the rod in time, goes unrecorded; I was probably immersed in yet another of the thousands of sci-fi books I have read avidly since I was a nipper.

The two rods I was using (there being room on the bank for only two), were baited with broad bean. Line was 11lbs. Platil Strong, the hooks, Speedbarbs, were size four.

4.00 p.m. dawned, with still no carp to show for all the nibbles I had been having, so I decided to go round to the far bank, to collect daphnia with which to feed my baby pond carp. Fortunately, as it turned out, the holes in the net I used were too large to catch the bugs adequately, so I settled for a couple of buckets of water with what denizens of the deeps I could muster.

On my way back to the car, I halted in No. 1 Swim to speak to a syndicate member who was preparing to leave. He mentioned that he had heard my buzzers sounding off for much of the day, to which I informed him that the roach and bream were messing me about, adding that the carp were hard. He pointed out that Jed and his mate had done alright the past couple of weeks. Brusquely, I agreed and took off for my car, thinking 'Two carp a summer do not make, mate'. I changed back into boots and sauntered, contentedly enough, back to my pitch.

At that time, I was still using antenna buzzers for audible bite indication and they had a habit of coming on and staying that way. I had disconnected them at the box to save battery waste and when I plugged in again, the buzzer box emitted its angry rasp, like a queen bee laying eggs with the sting on the outside. I pushed back the antennae of the heads, pulled the line through a shade to check everything was working O.K., then took my hands away, my eyes on the water, to hear a rattling sound. Looking down, I saw the rattling was caused by the indicator on one rod and the line was hissing out. I stepped back, closed the bale-arm and struck, finding myself playing a fish whose initial rush took it well away from the reeds. The fish veered to my right, catching the line on the reeds, so I held the rod well up and backwound as the carp plodded about out there, every now and then swirling on the surface. Although I could not determine whether it was large or average, I knew it wasn't small.

After a tense, sweaty period, my line was still in the reeds, thankfully running free, but I considered I would have to go in after the fish. Already up to my ankles in water, I struggled out of my jacket for the second time that season when fast into a fish, removed my watch and, remembering wet banknotes and drowned moths, my wallet. I threw the lot onto the bed-chair and marched in. By the time I was up to my waist in the briny the thought had struck me that I was going down too fast and if the mud impeding my progress was more than three feet deep, I would need a snorkel to reach the reeds. I didn't happen to have a snorkel handy right then and thought it might take too long to cultivate a set of gills, so regretfully I retracted my ponderous steps to dry land whilst I was still able.

The fish was allowed to take line in an attempt to coax him to the left and the reed-less gap I had cast through, but he wasn't having any. I couldn't persuade the line off the reeds by now and didn't have anything to throw at

Banks

P. Banks

Banks

P. Banks

the fish to scare him further away from the danger area, so the last alternative was to drag the carp through the reeds. Not unnaturally, I was by then wishing my trusty terylene was on the rod. After one last prayer, I held the rod as high as I could and reeled in slowly, letting the carp thrash his way through the reeds and into the clear water. Not a ploy to be undertaken lightly, I must say, but it worked. Drawing the fish to the net, I was sure all was won, but no, with a sudden regaining of his strength, he took line off the clutch I hadn't tightened down and bolted back out through the reed gap again! There was no other course now, but to clamp down and pull until the hook came away or the carp capitulated. Back through the gap he came and was netted first (or should it be second?) time. My prize was a lovely mirror of 24lbs. 12oz.

As if I wasn't in enough disarray already, I became muddier still photographing the fish and ripped my jeans at the knee as a bonus. But dirt and wetness are as nothing, when such providence is visited.

It was a further week before I visited the water again and the trip held a certain irony. Nige and I arrived together at 7.15 p.m. for a Friday nigh fling. I wasn't really concerned where I fished, so I let Nige decide where he wanted to go before making up my own mind. He chose the Moped. For old times' sake, I decided to fish the Special, setting up three rods. My most uncharacteristic malaise was further emphasised by the fact that I hadn't bothered even to bring any specials with me, satisfying myself with scrounging a handful of the inevitable Kit-e-Kat off Nige. I baited two rods with 'Kat' and a third with broad beans.

Cast in for 8.30, I had a lift on the vegetable rod within half an hour which I struck at and missed. At 9.30 the buzzer sounded on the left hand rod and I saw the line moving through the rings. With fingers trapping the line, I struck, felt the fish, then clicked over the bale-arm and tightened up to the fish which crashed out of the water – beyond the reeds in front of my position! Strangely enough, the fish came back through the reeds without too much trouble and moved about in the 'safe' area of the swim as though he wasn't going to fight. It was going to be one of those situations where although the fish is seemingly going to give up the ghost almost before it has started, you just can't align the net and fish. Try as I would, I couldn't net that fish. Round and round he went in the gloom, no doubt becoming dizzy on the way.

Eventually, though, the carp came close to the net once too often and I collared him before he could change his mind. Yet another fish had fallen to me in the Special and this one, weighing 17lbs. 4oz. had certainly given everything he had.

When the carp was examined in the morning light, we found a hook of the type Nige had been using, embedded solidly in a pectoral fin. He had lost a good fish at the net a month previously. We surmised that I had landed the same fish, so Nige felt a little better, knowing he had only foul-hooked a 17 pounder in the first place and not lost a properly hooked twenty.

Kit-e-Kat had become by now, Old Faithful, a name which is so descriptive of that particular brand of cat food. It wouldn't surprise me if that bait mixed with bran and eggs and boiled to make a special, or mixed with something like Weetabix for a paste, has caught carp from 95% of the carp waters in this country.

The 17$^{1}/_{4}$lb. fish was my last of the season from Mywater. I hadn't had a lot of fish, but it had all been great fun, which is all I ask. With the doubles I caught from other waters, I believe it was one of the most enjoyable seasons I have had since specialising in carp, back in the sixties. I didn't fish the water a great deal following that night in the Special, but I will end this season's notes with an incident which rather sums up what I often think my capabilities amount to in the carp world.

I was fishing the Rectangle one cold, windy night, casting to the right against the reeds, when during the early hours, a carp took the bait and instantly wrapped the line round the inevitable reed stems. I pulled and jerked the rod, hearing the carp splashing, and threw whatever came to hand in a vain try at making the fish move off and free the line. These ploys didn't work and it was not possible to reach the fish, so I attempted to move to the right between the nearest reeds and the bushes against them. I could only push my way a few feet before the tangle of greenery held me back, leaving me floundering around, just like the carp.

It seemed to me that it would be best to get further along the reeds without the rod encumbering me, so I wound right down to the fish and placed the rod on the reeds, starting into the jungle again. I didn't get very much further than on the first attempt and could hear the carp giggling at my incompetence, so, demoralised, I went back to the rod and picked it up. Well, at least I would have picked it up had it been where I thought I had rested it. No amount of searching in the pitch blackness (with no torch), produced the rod and still the carp splashed every now and then, just as a tease. Finally, I just had to call it quits and wait for the dawn.

When dawn arrived, I found the rod, lying on the reeds as large as life, just where I'd expected it to be. The carp, of course, had gone. It was only a little one, I reckon! It is no wonder that we begin, after a year or two of carp fishing, to mutter feverishly to ourselves.

This lost rod story really is true – except for the carp giggling, but if carp can, I reckon that one was.

* * *

CHAPTER 3

Fred

Three months of waiting, working, hoping, planning – scheming even. The close-season is all these things and more. It is painted on the canvas of the angler's life, just as is June 16th. The close-season is an integral part of our year: a time of re-evaluation, of telephone chats, buying tackle, making baits, rides to waters new and old, watching the quarry from the boughs of tall trees – gloating at the size of the carp. I do not believe that it is in the best interest of anglers or fish that the close-season should be abandoned. The three months is a long but most exciting period; a great build-up to the glorious day when all the new ideas and baits are put to the test. Whether failure or triumph comes along is by the way.

* * *

The pre-season visits to Mywater were taken up, in the main with throwing in yet more pound notes in the form of a new type of trout pellets Nige and I had acquired during April. We prepared the pellets by soaking them in hot water to form a mush, mixing with Farlene baby powder, flour and eggs and rolling into balls. 600 of these balls were boiled hard as an anti-sprat measure, whilst 200 were left uncooked. Over the four weeks before the season commenced we threw in the bait. It was the most expensive programme we have ever undertaken but we knew that this particular brand of T.P. had been catching a lot of carp, nationwide, so Nige and I considered the time and money spent would pay dividends. As observation proved that the carp were taking the bait well it is not hard to imagine that we were both getting excited as the golden day drew ever closer.

Despite my comments at the beginning of this new chapter, I am not one of those anglers who delays casting in until the local clock strikes midnight, but after landing the big one so soon after the start of the previous season we decided to wait until bang on midnight before casting out. We shouldn't have worried: the carp were spawning!

For a couple of days Nige and I let the carp get on with their nuptials. Although a couple of members carried on from the 16th only one fish was hooked, and that lost, up to the fourth day when, at midnight, I landed the same mirror from the Hidey Hole I had caught last year. Now 1¼lbs. heavier, at 26lbs., it fell to trout pellet bait, but otherwise circumstances and the fight were similar to the previous capture, so I will not bore the reader with another rendition! I was, needless to say, chuffed with this fish. Only once before had I had one equal to it in size.

During that first week the weather was really hot and the carp seemed to have given up feeding and taken up sunbathing, as I did for some of the time, whilst reading the ever-present sci-fi books. Swimming whiled away the hours, too, as well as walking round with carp rod in hand.

* * *

A hot and sticky trial is the stumbling around the lake. Hoping for feeding fish in this heat is akin to putting seven crosses on the pools coupon and expecting eight draws. The rod tip always seems to catch on the ground and bend double, throwing the butt-ringed hook off into the thicket; the net becomes impossibly tangled with the brambles, which I swear reach out when I'm not looking and grab a creeper full. When the other side of the lake is reached the realisation dawns that the bait bag is in the swim from whence I came, or the cigars have fallen out of the hole in my pocket and now, having tumbled and slid, lie down the slope of the bank in a farrago called a Swim, accessible only to a shrew or a Centurion tank. One thing, though: the mosquitos (those misanthropic gnats of the night, those raisers of bumps and suckers of blood) aren't around. No! They have more sense than to challenge the sun and let the horse-flies attack our skin. Geroff! Squashed bodies hanging on after the slap, with crushed, oozing proboscis embedded in the skin – a freckle of smeared green intestine to add to the thousand natural freckles already there.

Science fiction never dreamed of heroes like us, ready to suffer gallantly under boiling sun with broiling brains, merely hoping for a slate-grey shape to rise from the depths and pluck a piece of cake from the roof of their homes. Heroes like us, the sweat trickling into our eyes, combining with the sun's ferocious glare to half blind us; selling our souls to the lumps of flesh and bone we call carp.

* * *

A large carp began to make itself heard in the Rectangle, crashing over in the reeds once or twice a day. I christened him Fred, vowing that I would catch him before the summer was out.

Blunty.

We are all continuing to blank, then, in the second week of the season, one of the members actually landed another fish, a common of $14^{1}/_{2}$lbs., with no top lip. The fish, Blunt Nose, is caught up to six times a season and varies between 13 and 17 pounds. Most of my present syndicate have caught old Blunt Nose at least once.

In the early hours of the 24th I had a 12lb. leather, from the Special, on T.P. That fish had to work to get itself hooked: I was in one of my comas when the buzzer sounded, startling me awake. The silver paper indicator on the rod cast next to the sunken bush was up to the butt although it was no longer moving, so I pulled it back to ground level again, whereupon it sailed back up to the butt and gave me a beckoning wink whilst it waited for me to collect my sleep-addled wits. I did collect them, plus the carp as mentioned.

Falling asleep after dark is par for the course when I have been wandering about all day, climbing trees, hunting for something to throw a hook at. In any case, sitting for hours in a confined swim without so much as a twitch on the lines is a pretty boring hobby when God has put out the lights.

For everybody it was a slow season. A few carp were caught, of course; Nige had two or three doubles, one on crust fried in the chip-pan. Ginger caught a couple to 16lbs. I landed another one on T.P., but the larger fish seemed to have left the county.

I was trying hard to catch a Mywater carp on particle baits at this time, using various types of beans, but none seemed to interest the carp in the slightest.

I was again lucky when a $12^{1}/_{2}$lb. common hooked itself whilst I was on the other side of the water from my rods talking to Nige. This fish waited patiently, amongst the assorted snags and reeds of the New Swim until I got back to my rod and played it to the net.

I was using terylene hook lengths on one or two rods for much of the dead period, in the swims where the lighter nylon could be used, in an attempt to see whether the softer terylene would prompt fish to take baits. The links were about 15" long and tied to the end of the nylon with a double blood knot. As I was fairing badly with both set-ups I proved little, although in more favourable circumstances it is quite likely that the links could well out-fish plain much-used nylon.

September rolled in before I visited the lake again but I might just as well have carried on fishing other waters, I suppose, because I caught nothing at all.

Who cares about frustration? Frustration is wanting to sit in the water and cast onto the bank. It is the sum of the gremlins who lay their cold, unfriendly touch on you. Frustration is catching nothing when everything seems 'right'; crying bitter tears and gnashing brittle teeth in seething anguish – forever. Well not quite forever, because success comes if the work is continued and the waiting is patient.

* * *

Fred had continued to crash in the Rectangle reeds once or twice a day and I muttered to myself and the others that I **was** going to catch him. The Rectangle is cut off from the main body of water by reeds except for a gap 8' wide which allows the fish to move in and out. At this opening the water is something like 8' deep, gradually shallowing up to 3' deep against the grassy west bank, from which the area is generally fished. In the reeds near the south bank I found a patch of mud sparsely reeded and kept flat by the shuffling and snuffling of the carp. This patch I now call the Suicide Spot, due to the high chances of any carp hooked in it snagging the line and escaping. To fish it meant pushing through a gap in the thorns on the bank and sitting tight to the water's edge.

I had got into the habit of throwing a handful of small luncheon meat cubes into and around the Suicide Spot on odd occasions during my fishing sessions. Over a period of weeks I threw in several cans of the pink meat but only tried twice, a total of three hours, to catch the fish from there. These two attempts failed. The autumn nights were beginning to strike cold when I finally decided that I must make a serious attempt at catching Fred.

I set up the gear in the conventional position, fishing three baits, one cast into the middle of the Rectangle and two to the right where Fred always seemed to crash. As darkness cloaked the water I was, as ever, hopeful. I will let Fred take up the story…

"I am not one of those mind-reading carp the anglers talk about in their more heady moments, but merely a plump mirror, with little claim to special powers. The svelte females who court me in my reedy sanctuary appear impressed with my healthy mien, my courtesy in allowing them room to swim in the area I have made my own these past months. They seem taken with the way I have rooted out the tough reed stems, giving more room to turn than was found before. I in turn, am flattered to think that they should come all the way from their favourite areas across our watery home to visit me.

When males enter my domain I greet them, nuzzle them in a comradely fashion: it is not our way to be completely reclusive, even should we choose to remain alone for certain periods of the day. But the large brothers and sisters (nor the sprightly youngsters brashly scurrying through my palace) do not overstay their welcome, so for much of the time I am alone.

Being of a nervous disposition, I am happiest when surrounded by the reed stems, which, perhaps, is why I have not yet suffered the fate of my less wary contemporaries who often find themselves tethered to a slim length of 'line' and bundled, unceremoniously, into the air. The clearing I have made allows me to bask in the sun whilst still hiding me from anglers.

"Long ago I discovered that the irritating lice which gather on my skin to feast could be dislodged if I leaped out of the water and endeavoured to crash splashingly back. Thus, when the attentions of these parasites becomes too much to bear, I turn the water to foam and remove them from my skin, frightening off the small fish which dare to trespass; shaking the reed stems until the tiny buntings fly away in mortal terror. Of course, the anglers' interest is drawn in my direction, but I know that I am safe in my line-cutting hide.

For some time now I have regularly found a delicious crop of food sinking on to the muddy carpet of my home. At first I allowed the tiny, fearless roach and rudd to eat my food, but lately I have eaten all the strangely-shaped pieces and look for more coming down from the reed stalks. I patrol the reeds more often, now, looking for this food in the thicker sections of the reeds and in the deeper water along the border of the stems. Only today I have found, as well as a nice feast on my muddy patch, some odd foods scattered in the reeds. It is dark, now, but my sensitive barbules and the water sifting through my nostrils indicate that more of this food is to be found. Agh! There is a piece now..."

Thank you, Fred, for your side of things.

At 11pm the luncheon meat rod cast to the right against the reeds indicated a bite, with the silver paper shooting up to the butt ring and the rod sliding down the rests. I grabbed it and held on to the fish which at first reacted with the slowness of a carp befuddled and surprised at being hooked. Pumping and winding I brought the fish almost to the net before it shrugged off its apparent lethargy and realised it **was** hooked. The carp then swam so

Fred.

quickly away from me that I had to stop backwinding and use the clutch. It almost reached the 'entrance' to the main lake before I had enough pressure on to hold it. The fight then became easy enough, line being gained steadily until the fish was netted on the first attempt. Fred, caught at last, was a short, fat fish, with a fine display of big scales on its flanks and a figure which suggested he didn't visit any weight watchers club, the deepest fish I had had from Mywater – and the best looking!

Fred

Shining my torch into his mouth, I found the hook was well back near the throat, but it came away easily. As I adjusted the scales to zero on the weighing sack my anticipation was high and I was trembling with a kind of fulfilment I have rarely felt. This capture was like a dream on a bleak, fishless day. The veiled threats; the throwing in of the luncheon meat over a protracted period; the listening and speculating at the crashings he had regularly made in that reedbed – and now, a lovely fish on the bank, weight a solid 21lbs. 4oz. Had I died right then I would not have wished for a more satisfying end to life.

That was virtually the end of the season's excitement at Mywater for me. I fished after the capture of Fred, but the water continued to be difficult, except for odd doubles falling to one or two members.

The last carp I hooked that season, purely by accident, was in January.

The second day of the new year, a muggy drizzly day, saw me fishing for livebait in the Special Swim. About mid-day, the float-fished maggot cast alongside the sunken tree produced a bite, the float sliding across then under the surface. I struck and was fast into a surprise! A big fish had taken a fancy to the maggots and tugged a little at the rod. After a few seconds I saw, a foot below the surface, a double-figure carp. With one pull the fish moved off through the tree and the $2^1/_2$lb line went ping!

I caught a few roach and perch until nightfall, then settled down for a night's carping with the wind increasing in strength, blowing down to the end I was fishing. About 7pm came a nice, easy rise on the middle rod indicator, baited with sunken crust. The fish, when hooked, wriggled on the end of the line with no great gusto and came straight to the top, where I saw it was a daft 11lb. pike we had had more than once on our carp baits. I pulled it into the net, but while I was trying to disentangle it the pike kindly bit through the line and slid back into the water. The winds were now blowing with great force from my right and in the next two hours bite registration was a farce; my brolly was blown inside out twice so I took it down, whereupon it began to rain. The trees and bushes surrounding me were dancing the Rumba and I began to worry about my safety. At 9.15 I decided to get the hell out of there.

After I had put away the rods a small tree collapsed into the gap I had been fishing through. Could well be I would have needed some new gear had I been a hero and stayed put. On the way home the howling gale vented its fury on the landscape, with trees bending to breaking point, branches, grit, herbage flying across the roads as if they were being attracted by a gigantic magnet. Through the town newspapers, tin cans, plastic sacks, even a bottle crossed the path of my car, hurled blindly by the force of the wind. I ran over a three feet long branch on the way and wondered whether the rest of the tree would come out and get me.

The route I took home that night encompassed one of the city's main roads, along a section of which a mass of large trees had previously held their ground to all that the elements could throw at them, but, for some, that night was their last and the road was partially blocked with their carcasses. The flashing blue lights of the attendant police vehicles eerily lit up the chaotic scene as I crawled past. I read in the local paper the next day that at this spot not only trees but a man had died.

What, you may ask, went wrong with the trout pellet bait? A good question! Were we using the wrong formula of T.P. and additives! I do not really believe that is so, although others more knowledgeable about such matters could well nod wisely, thinking we did it all wrong. With a good deal of hard fishing behind the bait and only three fish on the bank, Nige and I consider we failed. I am not complaining about my 26 pounder, mind! The paradox was that in the close season I had firm evidence to indicate the carp were mopping up all the free baits within 24 hours of the baits being thrown in. Why the hook baits were treated with disinterest I know not.

There have been bad seasons at Mywater; sometimes I think the reasons are down to a better natural food supply for the year; then again it could be the carp have become so wary of the 10lb. line we **have** to use to land them. The terylene leaders I was using for quite a lot of the time did not seem to influence results at all. I am quite sure that were I to persist with leaders in a 'normal' season my rate of fish hooking could well go up. At least 15lb. terylene is **different.**

The final extract in the diary for the season reads: "Goodbye to the season. Not a bad one. Most ever doubles in a season and most ever twenties, if not from Mywater. Barrel Lake spoilt things in the summer, but I think I learned a lot – and enjoyed myself. Winter has been a bit rough as far as carp are concerned but I enjoyed the roach fishing a great deal. I will, no doubt, catch more Mywater roach next winter. But now there is the summer to look forward to."

* * *

CHAPTER 4

A Visit from Terry & Vampire Fishing

The previous August, the owner had decided he didn't want the bother of the water any more, as his business interests had cut down his fishing to one or two trips a year. I had, in fact, been running the syndicate since the previous close-season, so eventually he turned the water over to me, early in the New Year. I had realised the dream of every serious angler – a water of his own; a dream often cherished but not often brought to fruit. Mind you, I only had the place on a tenuous yearly rental.

I changed nothing with the syndicate, except to write down and issue the rules which had previously been word of mouth; all they insisted on, basically, was common sense and observation of the litter laws! I am rather proud of the fact that should anyone visit the water, at any time, they will only find the odd spent match on the bank – and that is the way it is going to stay.

Again, the gill nets and seine net were put to task; once more the so much smaller gill nets showing they could out-fish their big brother.

I visited the water several times just to watch the carp and their reaction to various concoctions I intended using, come the new season. On one such trip, I was observing fish in the Moped Swim, when I spotted a small oilslick on the surface. Underwater investigation resulted in a moped, complete with crash helmet on the handlebars, which had been rolled into the water. I hauled the vehicle out and left it on the bank, with a view to informing the local constabulary, but within a couple of days, the moped had gone. The name of the swim didn't, though. Funnily enough, I later found another moped thrown into a lake not too far from Mywater – must be something they put in the tea round that area.

This summer was to be my best ever season in numbers of carp caught, but not many of them were Mywater fish, I am afraid to say, where the going was hard – for me at least.

The first three fish, taken on the first three nights of the season, weighed $28^1/_4$lbs., 21lbs and 16lbs., all caught by Ginger from the Hidey Hole. Oz had a small double. I was blanking out elsewhere!

In the local Co-op just before going to the lake for the first time in the new season, I spotted a tin of mackerel pieces in brine. Always on the lookout for a new bait, I bought several tins and at home mashed up the chunks of fish and added flour and bran to make a paste. Asking Nige to smell it for me (the paste), he pronounced it to be similar to 'Kat', the bait he was still plugging away with but which I had more or less abandoned. Grey 'Kat' already! This paste received a great deal of attention from the sprats in the first two days I spent at the water, then the carp began to spawn. My new bait must have turned them on.

Nige had a 15lbs. 10ozs. common on the 21st, but I wasn't around as I never rate the water when the carp are doing their yearlies.

I went down on the 23rd, depositing mackerel baits in various swims and casting in now and then when a carp looked as though it might be interested in a snack. The only fish to dare take a bait promptly had it struck out of its mouth. I was consoled by the nature of the day, though, it being yet another scorcher. The birds were whistling to their hearts content and the midges and bees hurtled around my head as if there was no tomorrow. Even the whirligig beetles, clustering together in their little watery communes, seemed to be whizzing round in circles more rapidly than usual: the water was so hot it was burning their feet.

To finish off the day, I joined the whirligigs for a swim round the lake, the other anglers having either gone home, fallen asleep or melted into puddles. Only momentarily did the water seem chilly to my hot skin as I waded in from the Special Swim, my few clothes lying crumpled and lonely on the bank. Soon I could appreciate the warmth of the water and glided past the old, sunken tree, which shed thin clouds of detritus and algae as my passing moved the branches. Sometimes swimming, often pulling myself along by the reeds, I visited the Plateau and walked in the gait of an astronaut on the surface of the moon, pushing the light weed around with my feet, the water just touching my chin.

In the Hidey Hole, I stirred up the thick mud as I removed dead branches from the bottom. No doubt my friends would have told me that the disturbed mud stank, but I was not able to make the distinction twixt sweet or bad and nosed past the bush and through to the Little Tree Swim, then to the Swamp, grasping the thick reed stems and pulling them clear from the bottom which their roots gripped as fiercely as a tiger its prey. The sun beat down as I worked and all was calm and right with the world. Would that every day could be the same. It was not many days before I was back again.

The bank was overgrown again in the Twenty Swim but, during the previous week, I had cleared the end of the big branch which came away from the old willow and allowed me to sit six feet above the water and to dangle a bait into the swim.

At 10.00 a.m. a small double nosed its way into the swim and immediately sucked in the mackerel special lying amongst the thinly scattered reeds. I struck and the bait, now squashed flat, came back. 'That'll teach me to boil the baits too hard', I mused. Another fish later came and admired the bait but showed no inclination to take it. I watched him as he drifted off and felt the line pulling from between my thumb and forefinger; yet another fish had swiftly nipped in, picked up the bait and headed east, like a bat out of hell. I didn't hook that one either.

The next bait was carefully placed just past the reed fringe, where the bottom drops off almost vertically into 8 feet of water. Soon, the line tightened up; I struck and was into a fish which bolted to my left, taking the line, so I dropped the landing net on to the reeds and myself into three feet of muddy, weedy, water. I waded the few feet to the weed fringe but although the fish was almost next to me, I couldn't net it, as the branch was in the way. Shaking the branches scared the carp into a headlong rush which I couldn't halt until it was almost across the bay. Like many a fight with carp, the big effort of a long run under pressure, was enough to take the wind out of its sails and I netted the fish shortly after I had pumped it back. Following the licking I had taken the first two weeks of the season, that carp, at 15lbs. 12ozs., was a very welcome sight.

The reader will have observed that I seldom state why I fish certain swims at certain times, apart from the observation of carp. This is because Mywater is all about the observation of the fish, rather than following weather conditions, though when the wind is strong enough to affect the surface, some carp will often follow it: this latter, of course, is 'standard' carp fishing knowledge. I think, too, there is an instinct in fishing the right spot, gained over years of fishing, but this is not so easy to describe: you know of certain spots where it makes sense the carp will use as a route, like a yard wide gap between the reeds and a large bed of hornwort, or they will visit an area covered with debris which appears not to have been disturbed for a long time, except for one small patch. Baits go on that patch. Discoloration of the water is a good guide to finding carp but at Mywater the general colour of the main lake area is fairly muddy, with little variation, except on rare occasions such as during the winter and at spawning time, when the water clears.

I fished Elliott's Swim the day after I had caught the fifteen pounder from the Twenty and suffered much movement of the lines, which I deduced was mainly large fish bumping into the line (line bites); striking proved a waste of time. I was cast into the Gap at this time. The Gap has always been an enigma; it often seems tenanted by the carp but seldom, and with no obvious pattern, do they feed in it. We assume that periodically a good item becomes available in sufficient quantity to tempt the carp to eat, although heavy baiting by the angler does not seem to motivate the carp into feeding there. Like the proverbial stubborn mule, the Gap carp move when they feel like it. Plainly, this day they were feeding, but not on my baits.

You can fish the Gap and have a carp within minutes of casting in; you can bait up and wait, and wait, and bait up some more and wait until the carp finally turn up. It was to the latter end that I baited up the Gap with Gunga beans and fished for more than two days and nights, pushing in more beans as the mood took me. Without a bite and with fish everywhere else, seemingly, I finally capitulated. Fishing is for fun and despite my books, I was dying of boredom.

Heavy baiting with particles is a sure way of encouraging roach to feed but I am not very interested in catching $^1/_2$lb. roach on ten pound line. I think a carpet of beans would work in the Gap, were somebody patient enough to sit out the wait and put up with the sprats – or lucky enough to drop on the fish straight away. The day after I had abandoned the Gap, Nige landed a 17 pounder from there, hooked fairly in the bum! Some time later, he had Fred take in and spit out a crust in the Twenty Swim, fishing the end of my branch. My swims soon become popular!

* * *

Hazy, lazy times. Full of sun in the day, the sharpness of the stars at night. Which dot of light in the velvet sky is Venus? Is that one over there Mars? The Plough sits over the Middle Swim. Or is the Plough a non-stick pan? More like a pan than any old plough. Lights flashing, a U. F. O., better known as an aeroplane, drones high above, going on its dark, mysterious journey, the pilot unaware his night-ship is being watched by a pair of ever-seeing brown eyes. The nose grows cold – breathing vigorously into cupped hands slowly warms it.

Sprats dapple the surface at dawn, their disturbances and the swirling mist making intricate patterns for me to watch in wonder. The rare sight of a kingfisher; gorgeous plumage flashing in the rising sun as it heads in its direct, no nonsense flight to the end of the lake: its fishing is to sustain life – mine just for pleasure. And pleasure indeed does it bring me.

Elliott in Elliott's Swim.

I went snorkelling one day and witnessed, on the Plateau, one of the most beautiful sights I have seen since taking up fishing. I was slowly swimming along, my head under the water, when a shape came towards me and halted, at the same time as I, a few feet away. It was a double figure carp and every detail of the fish was highlighted by the bright sun shafting through the water. The tiny bubbles on the fish's flanks were crystal clear; a gold and silver line was the silhouette. The tone of the skin was silken; the barbules waving as the carp's mouth opened and closed. Then he turned and was gone, more quickly than he had appeared. I can still see that vision, years later, as clearly as if it were yesterday. I look forward to the day when I can purchase the proper equipment for underwater fish spotting, then my close-seasons will be spent doing just that; learning more about my love and taking photographs over which to dream in the dark, dank winter months.

The next swimming session was an impromptu dip when I fell, fully clothed, into the Rectangle. Never slow to miss out on opportunity, I cleared out some more reeds in Fred's home whilst I was there. Those reeds keep on growing, don't they?

On Sunday, August 1st., Terry Eustace came to fish the night at Mywater. I had already been using the set of T24 rods I had bought as kits in the close season (catching fish on them, too, in other waters) and Terry brought with him a new one to add to my collection. It had my name neatly printed on it too!

Now I am not what you would call tackle proud and the rods I used then – if the rings weren't actually stuck on with insulating tape – were whipped on my way. That is to say I had perfected a technique of using two bobbins of thread at a time to secure the rings, thereby doing the work in half the time. I was quite pleased with my effort, but I could see by the tears in Terry's eyes, when he saw the job I made of his kits, that he wasn't impressed! Sign of a good tackle-maker that. Seeing as I was letting him fish a water few are allowed to, Terry was too polite (or diplomatic) to make too much of my rod building.

At the water, I suggested the swims he might fish and the bait he could use and he took it from there, fishing in the Mud Swim and casting to the Gap with diced luncheon meat as bait.

These Brummy anglers have a strange ritual when fishing, you know. They fry bacon sandwiches, then scald a few fingers by pouring boiling fat over them. The ritual seems to work though, because shortly after 10.30 p.m., as I sat talking to him, he had a twitch or two, then a slow rise of the indicator on the luncheon meat baited rod and was fast into a fish. Giving the fish more stick than I would ever dare do in the 'safe' pitch (at least it is safe once the fish is in front of you), Terry made short work of the job and the carp was soon in the net. At 16lb. 4oz. it was a good initiation to the water. I never actually elicited from Terry whether he always likes to separate the head from the body.

I fished the Rectangle all night. Being tired, I went into a coma, waking only once, to hear somebody shout – it was me!

In the morning, Terry showed me another fish – a 20lb. 2oz. mirror! That was the only time that season two double-figure carp were caught in the same session. What might Eustace have caught had he stayed the week?

The day after the Brum double, I also fished the Gap. After unhittable twitches for hours, I struck into a fish at 4.40 a. m., just as dawn was waking up the world around me, and duly landed a common of 12$^1/_2$lb., to the rod Terry had presented to me two days before, funnily enough. Like a fool, I pushed in some baits and fished a further three nights into the Gap – Tuesday, Thursday and Friday – and didn't get a decent bite. They probably went mad on the Wednesday night!

One day I was at the lake, having taken my wife for a ride and some fresh air (isn't it funny how anglers' cars always head for water when the family desire to see the countryside?), when we both spotted a big, fat fish slowly cruising through the New Swim. I estimated its weight at about thirty pounds, the largest fish I had seen in the water. Imagine my delight when, following yards behind, swam an even bigger fish! During all the hours I have spent at Mywater, I have never before or since seen those two carp as far as I am aware.

On the Monday, a week after Terry's trip, Pete Hall's father, with whom I worked, came rushing around before starting time (and me with sleep still in my eyes and brain), to breathlessly inform me that Pete had caught a big one on Saturday lunch time. Pete later told me that he was climbing along the branch to my tree access above the Twenty Swim, when a large caterpillar dropped out of the tree and landed next to him. He put the grub on the hook and, once in position above the swim, dangled it against the leaves of a lily plant I had put in there during the close season. Soon, a big fish took the bait and after a battle royal, it was landed. At 31lb., it beat the previous water record by a clear three pounds. What a fish!

The 18lb mirror with a taste for blood.

It was August 20th before I fished Mywater again; one in a long line of Friday-nighters. I set up in Elliott's Swim around 7.00 p. m., tying half-bloods, forcing in rod-rests, organising things so that gear I had saved for wouldn't be ground into the dirt after dark, because it was in a stupid position.

Oz, being of a sadistic bent, shoots ducks and hares and such things when he isn't fishing, and that day he had kindly brought me a nice hare, ungutted, which I cleaned before setting off for the lake. Observing the cold, dark blood in the bowl I dropped the intestines into, I drained the blood off and mixed it with a loaf of dry bread. That was one of the baits for the night, cast into the Plateau. Two other baits, cheese cube and luncheon meat cube, were cast into the Gap.

Not unusually for me, I was tired, and dozed a while until a buzzer stirred me and I mustered spirit enough to move the baits around a little. I lost the bomb on one rod so I put a crust pad on the hook, moulded a dollop of the rather gooey blood paste on and cast it out to the Plateau. Within a short while I had a twitch or two on the blood bait and the indicator began to rise gently. I struck and hooked the fish which, no doubt charged with the blood, fought for some time on the ten pounds bs. line. Twice in the five minutes the fight lasted, I had him near the net, only to grudgingly give line as he powered off. Eventually, though, he just had to capitulate and I lined him up with the white-painted arms of the landing net for the third time and this time, got it right. That fish was a well scaled mirror of just 18lb. The rest of the night passed with no more luck.

I had caught a Mywater upper double on a bait which had not been used before on the water and I had plenty left by the time the session was over, so I decided to try it on the water again, instead of going, as I had planned, to another water. I blanked! Oz was due to bring me a rabbit on the Wednesday so I decided to give that animal's haemoglobins a run-through on the next Friday night trip, but Oz didn't manage to get one, so I fished without blood on my hands. I blanked! Nigel had a $13^1/_4$ pounder the day before and one of $18^1/_4$lb., the day after. From my point of view, I was tempted to wonder if the carp had been posting look-outs at the bottom of the lane this season.

I ventured to the water again, on the Sunday night, this time with my eldest boy. After seeing Jason (better known as Jay) tucked up warmly in my spare bed-chair, I fished on through the wet, warm night and again blanked. I blanked too, on the following Wednesday night.

17lb leather off the plateau.

They go on and on, these blanks, don't they? Perpetual nothings for me to record in my tear-stained diary. The green-glowing bobbins lie motionless an inch from the ground for hour after gloomy hour. Sleep comes, perhaps, creeping into the mind, levelling the breath into a shallow rise and fall of the chest.

But sleep isn't always the way of escape.

No brolly camp for me. No brolly, even if privacy or inclement weather do not dictate it. Just an unfettered view of the dark world where my thoughts roam until my eyes look, as always, upwards.

Above, lost in the endless, black confusion of space, lie planets revolving round hot, alien suns. Planets I, regretfully, will never see. How many times, whilst sitting on my bed-chair, have I wondered if there is anything 'out there' worthy of the adjective – intelligent? Is there anything to compare with what an earthly carp angler does? Are there sentient beings sitting still as the grave by the side of excavations filled with a mix of hydrogen and oxygen, waiting their lives out for a mass of bone and nerve tissue to take in its mouth a ball of protein? Do these sentients, should they exist, sit and wonder, just as I do?

My thoughts plummet back to earth as a chilling yell escapes from the spinney to my rear. The vixen – perhaps attracting her mate, or gloating over the steaming corpse of a luckless rabbit. So too, do the owls screech, sending the iciness of death into the heart of an innocuous shrew. And all the time the stars watch down on us in stony silence; atomic furnaces from which we will never feel the heat but of which I always dream.

* * *

Something keeps us tolerating the blanks, though. Instead of giving up as a bad job, a seemingly hopeless situation, we keep grinding on. What **could** I do to stop the rot that had, for the most part, flattened my catches at Mywater that summer? Hand grenades were considered. They do a good line in harpoons at the chandlers down the road. If I had not been catching so well elsewhere that season, I would probably have given up carp fishing and entered a monastery.

Grudgingly, the water was giving me just enough to keep me clocking on and the next Friday night, again with Jay in tow, and again in Elliott's Swim, produced a fish of 17lb. Lord above! This fish was a hard fighting leather which took a spicy sausage bait just before 4.00 a. m., on the Saturday morning. The worst stage of the fight came when, after a fouled-up netting attempt, the net swam off attached to the line and the carp underneath it! I managed to keep hold of the net handle but of couple of scoops showed that it was impossible to net the carp and the line wouldn't budge from where it was trapped between a net arm and the aluminium strip which forms one half of the spreader. Luckily, by the time I had got myself into the pickle, the carp was whacked and I did eventually free the frayed line and net the fish. Why I was persisting with the swim is not quite clear in my head, or my diaries! The number of bites I had had which **could** have been cagey carp were enough to keep me going back to that swim; that and the lure of the enigmatic Gap. The blood I was draining from the corpses Oz brought me were making paste baits which the tench had acquired a taste for. Blood being a traditional tench attractor merely suggested that my tench were keeping up with tradition.

On the 9th September, again at 4.00 a. m., I hit another fish on sausage paste, which fought like a 2lb. tench all the way to the net (not very well!), whereupon it waved a magic wand and turned into a (sheepish-looking) 16lb. common.

The last carp I landed from the lake that slow, frustrating season, was on Monday, September 13th. The day before, I had had my first lay-in since the season had begun three months earlier. I wanted to be fit for the night session at Mywater, so I luxuriated in a proper sleep and a soft, warm bed, not arriving at the water until 3.00 p. m. I fished off the Island, tackling up in the rain, which thoughtfully stopped just before dark. Nige came down after dusk and set up in Elliott's Swim. So much for being fit and fresh for the night shift. I was carp-less when the birds sang out their chorus at dawn. So too, was Nige.

As is my custom in the daylight hours, I reeled in my base station rods and wandered round the pit, searching the swim for carp. In the Little Tree Swim, I found several fish to eighteen pounds or so but I had to go back to the Island as I had omitted to drag any tackle round the lake with me! I chose a T24 rod with 10lb. main line and fifteen pounds terylene leader, saying to Nige, who was packing up, that I was going to waste my time on some fish I had spotted in the Little Tree. Normally I would have said I was going round to pull out two or three fish before lunch, but even my ever-optimistic attitude had been eroded to the point where it was looking decidedly frayed around the edges. I settled for a 32" landing net and toddled back to the north side, thinking that the carp would be soon swimming away, with sardonic grins on their faces.

Having negotiated the sloping bank, scratched my face on the brambles and stung an ankle on a gaggle of mischievous nettles, I soon had a 5p-sized piece of sausage paste lying against a clump of reeds in the channel of the Little Tree Swim. Wondering whether to rub my sore ankle, check my face for blood, or light a cigar, I was deterred from all such courses by the sight of a nice carp which drifted into view, mooched around in the open water for a while, then had the cheek to swim away again without even seeing the bait. As the fish had shown interest in the silt of the clear area, I reeled in the paste until it sat in full view in the middle of the channel. Carp often visit the same spot more than once during a period of hours and I guessed he would be back. Sure enough, within half an hour, the same fish swam into sight, studying the clear bottom. It soon spotted the paste and was down on it fast, sucking it in – then out again before I could strike! I cursed my sloth as it turned as if to depart, then smiled to myself as he turned again and sucked in the bait once more, in little eddy of silt. I reacted quickly this time and struck, with all of seven feet of line between rod tip and hook! The overhanging bush to my left, soon had a carp boiling under it, but, with the rod tip in the water, I hung on grimly until he decided to run along the channel, going to the right this time. I couldn't hold the fish, but applied heavy pressure until he reached the bush separating the Little Tree from the Hidey Hole, then, throwing caution to the winds, I had to clamp down and once more the carp boiled under the bush; I didn't expect to get that fish out from the bush, with its accompanying snags and reeds, but suddenly, my pulling hand had the desired effect and the fish came towards me, finishing, happily, under the rod.

Getting the 32" net through the clinging tree branches and into the water caused my concentration to lapse and the fish somehow became entangled with a clump of those damn reeds, just out of reach, and I could not budge it. So now I had to extend the screw-locking landing net pole with my left hand whilst waving the rod in the air with my right; again, I did the impossible, although this took a little longer. The first attempt at netting resulted only in an agitated fish, but this caused the line to clear the reeds. I drew the fish over the net and breathed that oft' heard sigh of relief.

I carried net, carp, rod and bait bag all back to the Island and the scales. Nige had gone so I had to congratulate myself on the size of the fish, another eighteen pounder. I was, needless to say, highly pleased with myself at pulling a good carp from that most miserly of swims.

Effective fishing at Mywater ended there; my interest in other waters, well to the fore that summer, took over completely.

* * *

CHAPTER 5

Of Gravel and Dog Meat

In the previous close season I had had reason to be rude to a shady character I found snooping round the water. I tend to become aggressive when my patch is invaded by strangers who have no right there. Consequently, I conveyed this to the chap with my bellicose manner. The shady person, Graham Osborne, went away without too much argument. He told me, months later, he thought on our first meeting, the stories he had heard about me were true; perhaps they are. I got to know 'Oz' later in the summer when we were both fishing another water and realised that he was a nice chap who would make a good member of the syndicate, so by September, he was fishing Mywater twice a week and took up full membership for this season. Now Oz and I are very good friends.

As Oz's interest in the water was sufficient to stand some punishment, I got him to help me clear the outlet stream during the winter – a job much needed but long-delayed. We spent two days digging the stream out, right back to the hole in the ground where the water mysteriously disappears. The job was hard and messy, as years of accumulated twigs, leaves, weeds and rubbish had combined to block up the outlet to an unacceptable degree. We hoped to drop the water level a further foot or so, but a large, gnarled tree root growing right across the mouth of the stream, reduced this to a mere six inches.

Two close-season schemes took a little organising, but kept me off the streets for a time. The first entailed throwing in gravel; I had decided to put a couple of patches of it on the Plateau to give a clear area on which to fish the baits, so, with the help of the syndicate members, 10 tons was slid down the bank in the Special Swim, bagged up and taken to the designated spot in a boat. We chose two spots for the gravel, both on the Plateau – one in front of the reeds by the Hidey Hole and the other near to the east end of the Plateau where the water drops off into the Gap.

That much gravel sounds a lot, but it is surprising how much is needed to form a solid base over three or four inches of weed. After several hours of sweating, mickey-taking and horsing about, we had two decent areas which, it was hoped, would be attractive, eventually, to the carp. I later spaded a little gravel into the Special Swim, forming a yard wide 'pathway' into the deeper water. The two patches of gravel on the Plateau have not appeared to affect catches a great deal, although carp have come from baits on or near to them. Half the trouble is accurately placing baits on the gravel 'bar'. The gravel in the Special **has** enabled more than one syndicate member to hook fish he

Ian Suttie and the nineteen.

might not otherwise have done.

The second scheme was to bait the water with a special. The syndicate undertook to bait up with Bounce dog meat, which was made into balls with the usual chick-feed, flour and eggs and boiled. Several hundred of these baits were put in the water over the last few weeks of the close-season. During the season, Bounce accounted for more carp than any other bait – hardly surprising.

The swim opposite the Gap was finally given its name – Elliott's Swim – after I did the necessary hard work to make it comfortable. As a reward for my labours, I claimed that swim for a period after the season began. This pitch, I'll have you know, even had a carpet (but not a red one) to the Mud Swim, but the carpet has now been hidden by the tramp of countless muddy boots. I should have named this pitch the Mosque, then everyone would have been obliged to take their boots off before setting foot in it. The Mud Swim gradually became defunct as Elliott's Swim gave better access to the areas which interest us. Now the Mud Swim is used solely for sacking carp.

The dawn of the new season, saw me arriving at 6.00 p. m. on the 15th., eager to do well, with a pile of baits not much smaller than the pile of groceries. The high hopes I had were slightly shot at as I didn't catch anything during the first two days!

Ian Suttie, a new member of the syndicate, caught the only fish of the first three days – and nights – a 12lb. 12oz. mirror.

During opening night, Bert Chambers, another new member, lost a double in the Special. The following night, Oz lost one from the Hidey Hole. Not to be outdone, on the third morning I hooked and lost a carp from the bottom of the Gap and Kev Maxfield lost one in the Rectangle. What a bunch of star carp anglers!

The most enduring memory of the gravel-shifting day had been Bert's fractured rendering of "I'm a lumberjack and I'm O.K." I reckon we should have taken up the sport of tree felling in line with his song and left the carp to competents.

On the Saturday, Oz, Ian and myself took a few hours off to see how a couple of other waters were faring and then drove back to Mywater and fished the night. Kev went one up on the rest of us during the evening by losing his second carp, again in the Rectangle.

To let the rot leave my system, I fished elsewhere for a few days, missing out on Ian landing his second carp of that first week, a lovely common of

19lb. I did, however, get roped in to take the pictures.

On the 25th., I risked a night's fishing. Nigel, coming down just after dark, landed a big one on P.Y.M. bait from No. 1 Swim in the night. The fish was Fred, weighing in at $23^{1}/_{4}$lb. Later in the season, Fred was looking very sorry for himself in the branches of the Special Swim sunken tree, and a few days after that I found him dead, floating on the surface in the Special. Sadly, Fred would give no one else the pleasure of his capture.

As well as not being a manual on carp fishing techniques, I had not intended it to be a book of blanks either (you might not have guessed), so the blanks, unless of significance, have merely been given a mention in passing. The following, however, must be put in this book as it is a cracker! Up to Monday, June 26th., I had had only one double from another water. The signs were that this season was going to be a repeat of the last at Mywater and I was not very pleased!

I arrived at the water with a ton of gear, intending to fish for the week. Every year I allow myself up to four days solid fishing, the rest of the season being spent in one and two day sessions, or short trips of a few hours' duration – "Put the kettle on, I'll be back soon" – so that my family are not too neglected. Work? What's that? The gear took a long time to transport round to Elliott's Swim, but at least it wasn't raining, as it had tended to do since the season started. The weather was continuing cold and the water temperature was a grizzly 59° F. Almost winter carping! The cold weather at least precluded the carp spawning, which was a blessing. The evening and night passed quietly, even the heavily baited Bounce specials did not interest the fish. Pete Hall fished the Island from dawn.

I spent three hours with two rods in the Rectangle, tempting nothing, then waded in (shiver, shiver) up to my waist, to clear the reeds, which had thickened again since the last time I had seen to them. Despite the coldness of the water, I wanted to even the chances of landing something should I hook it, so the devil drove where the must needed. When I stepped into the water I scared out a double and as I was pulling out reeds, the same fish came to see what all the fuss was about. It's all down in the diaries, isn't it? Do you want to know what I had for lunch that day? Perhaps not.

At 5.30 in the afternoon, Pete had a mirror of 13lb., casting into the New Swim from the Island. Before that I had a reel-spinning pike, a foul-hooked pike and, to end with a flourish, a reel-spinning carp which contrived to shoot through the rods and cut the line. Great! The weather had been cloudy for most of the day, with a still westerly breeze blowing into the Moped swim. The rain didn't come down in more than a few spots at a time, so at least something was partly right with the world as dusk covered the lake with its dark cloak. That night proved to be a blank as well; yet another nail in my coffin.

* * *

...Indefatigable, untiring, unremitting. That's what we are. And crackers, of course. Let the people who think anglers are fellows who sit for a short while watching floats dancing on sunlit waters, come down to the carp ponds, the tench lakes, the catfish lagoons. They might think we are nuts but they will have to concede we are dedicated! I think we want our heads seeing to, but the love is so strong for the sport I am still battering away after countless happy and sad days. Still battering away...

* * *

Various members of the syndicate fished over the next few days, catching only a couple of the small commons I had introduced the year before. The nearest I came to hitting a carp was when a mirror of about twelve pounds went down to a bait in the Swamp. In my eagerness to hook a fish, I struck too soon and the carp bolted.

As ever, I wandered about the water, rod in hand, as I have always done since discovering the lake, but there just was not a lot to see in the way of carp. I was seriously considering going by the middle of the week. That or suicide, but I had booked a week off work and I was blowed if I'd suicide on holiday. Syndicate members who came down in the week reported that other local waters were producing little, so I gritted my teeth and fished on. On Friday afternoon, I did give it best and left for home, a broken man – well, perhaps not broken but decidedly curled round the edges. It's great, isn't it, when the highlight of the week is a water temperature rise of 2° F. Still, Pete fished three more mornings after he had had his double and he blanked too, so I wasn't the only joker in the pack.

Whilst I snuggled up in bed that night, Oz fished No. 1 Swim and had a 13 pounder. The Saturday was the hottest day of the year with the sun blazing down from a cloudless sky. This started the carp spawning! Ian landed a fish of 16lb., from the Rectangle, on the Monday, so I decided to have

Two nice commons.

another shot at Mywater.

I reached the water late on Tuesday night, having played in a cricket match during the evening (we were thrashed by over a hundred runs! Just not my month), and tackled up in the Hidey Hole after a look round. The sky had clouded over again, but the rain held back. Using Bounce specials and sausage paste I was plagued with the sprats all night.

At dawn, I cast out once more. Lord above! A run came, on the Bounce special, which was slow enough for even me to hit. The fish moved to the left, the line against the reeds, but it did not fight very hard and within a minute was dragged through the gap in the reeds to the net. The prize was a common of 15lb. 3oz. I was pleased I could still tell commons from mirrors, etcetera! The water temperature, after so long in the doldrums, was now 70° F. The coldness of the water the previous week may have caused the fish to take cover until it warmed up, but it is possible that they were waiting, full of spawn and milt, disinterested in food, until they could explode into their yearly ritual. Certainly the carp spawned on that Saturday and then they began to be caught. I felt better at once.

The skies cleared around 9.00 a. m., the sun bathed the lake and I went walkabout, trying for a short while in the Rectangle and the Special before sitting back in the Hidey Hole and continuing the book I had been reading. About 1.45 I again went for a walk and saw some fish in the Moped Swim, with a couple lying under a raft of dead reeds in the far left corner of the swim, against the Island.

Being partial to honey, I usually have a jar in my bag when I fish for lengthy periods, so I decided to put some on the crust I intended presenting to the two carp across the Moped Swim. I crept round to the most accessible spot and lowered a thumb-nail sized piece of honeyed crust very gently between the two basking carp. The hook-heavy crust promptly sank! I pulled it up and balanced it on the surface debris, watching the two fish all the time. After a while, they had the gall to swim away, leaving me somewhat miffed. I moved the crust towards the edge of the patch of reeds, where the water gently lapped, and waited patiently again.

Soon, several carp had moved back and forth in the vicinity of the bread until one, a common, took a quick look at the bait and sucked it in without so much as a by your leave. Because of the vegetation which surrounded me, in the shape of wild rose and a couple of leafy saplings, I was restricted in playing space and the fish did much as it liked, finally snagging the line in the reeds. The fish was not strong enough to break the line, or its hold on the reeds and, the line for once not being cut, the fish lay where it was, looking at me as if to say, "Well, come on in and rescue me." Trouble was that the landing net wouldn't reach far enough, so I had to get wet. I had little to shed before going into the water up to my chin because I had been wearing only carpet slippers and underpants (due to the heat and not because I've got any strange inclinations). A few paces took me within netting distance and I gently slid the net under the tethered fish and lifted – claiming my second double of the day. I bit through the line by the reed, accidentally taking in a mouthful of water, threw the rod on the bank and waded after it.

The common weighed 13lb. 9oz., a size held almost in contempt by some 'anglers', but I had enjoyed catching it as much as many a larger carp.

The rest of the day was spent reading in the bed-chair, swimming and mooching around in the hopes of spotting carp – the latter being the least fruitful of the three options. Oz came down in the evening to spend a couple of hours tench bashing – he caught two bream and a roach!

In the Hidey Hole for the night, I had a belting run at 2.00 a. m., on a pilchard paste bait. I struck and felt nothing, but kept winding and eventually felt the fish. I had cast the bait almost to the Rectangle reeds, so deduced the carp had run towards me when it had picked up the bait. It kept running to the right and almost inevitably the nylon tangled with the reeds, despite a tight line and the rod held above my head. Ever gone in after a carp, at two in the morning, stark naked? Not a pretty sight!

I knew by now that I could walk in the Hidey Hole swim without sinking too deeply into the mud, so I confidently stepped in, having divested myself of my togs. Striving to keep a tight line, I beat a way to the reeds, swearing at the coldness striking my skin. Standing, finally, on the ridge of clay the reeds thrive on, the water now only lapping against my knees, I was able to shake the line off the reeds and play the fish in the normal manner. The fish fought back so hard that I was beginning to think I had hooked one of the big ones.

Once more, the line became snagged, this time on the reeds to my right, near the big willow, but I overcame that problem by lifting the rod high again and it seemed that the fish was ready. Soon, the carp was netted and I saw it was not as big as I had thought whilst playing it. It was an interesting episode, getting back to dry land without the fish swimming back out of the net, whilst remaining on my feet in the thick mud, but I made it, eventually, and was soon weighing the fish. I was muddy and my teeth were chattering but I was certainly happy with the hard fighting seventeen pounder. I slipped it in a keep sack.

I dried off, somehow, using weighing sacks, tissues – anything that came to hand, then dressed myself and went for a jog up the lane to warm my cold body!

I stayed at the water a further biteless day and night, then packed up and went home. There was, seemingly, a Civil Defence exercise in town that day, with everyone on my route home wearing gas masks. My wife hadn't got on a gas mask, but she put a peg on her nose and ran down to the other end of the street as I arrived. A scrawled note on the mantelpiece informed me that the bath was running and could I leave out some money for another bottle of Domestos?

That Friday night, I took my beloved to see Barbara Streisand in 'A Star is Born' – a lovely film, which very much appealed to the romantic in me. At the end, with a young lady almost in hysterics in the row in front, there was not a dry eye in the house. I just don't seem to be able to get away from water for five minutes, do I!

After the film, I took Jay with me to Mywater. The night was a blank for four of us. The other three anglers left before Jay and I, so I scattered some Gunga beans in one or two spots.

The colour of the water, summertime, is always of a constant muddiness in the main part of the lake, unless the carp are spawning, when it clears. I noticed that the darkness of the water was more pronounced in No. 1 Swim, gradually thinning out to normal about halfway along the Plateau. As my religion only allows fishing on Saturday nights on very rare occasions, I could not give the swim a try. Pity about that! During Saturday evening, Kev came round to tell me he had landed a mirror of 26¼lb. from No. 1 Swim, where he had settled shortly after I had gone home. The fish was sacked and he was going back for the night, so I agreed to take some photographs. Some of my family, plus Oz joined me early the next morning for the photographic trip.

When Kev's big fish was taken from the retaining sack, with it were the skins of Gunga beans which I evinced the carp had regurgitated during its period of imprisonment. Particles (small baits such as beans, etc.) are a far from easy way of catching Mywater carp; given the choice of baits, the carp almost invariably go for paste or specials. I have watched the fish take their pick on more than one occasion and the many different types of particles fished at Mywater over the years have been, for the most part, ignored. I suppose I must have spent a lot of money on these ole beans with little result, but I still hope for the day when I can coerce the carp into feeding heavily on a blanket of small baits and perhaps catch several in a sitting. That they have taken bean baits goes without saying, as witness Kev's big fish, but when I've got 'em (beans) on the hook, the Mywater carps' attitude to particles is outstanding only for its apathy!

It was September before I was on the bank again with more than a few hours to spare. Meanwhile, a sprinkling of fish had been landed, including the first ever twenty plus common (21lb. to Nigel) and England had won back the Ashes. I love the Tests against the Aussies so my radio had been working overtime during fishing.

Only one or two (blank) sessions are recorded for September and October until the end of the month when I hooked, on a Bounce special, and landed a mirror of 19lb., which did not fight too well on 15lb. bs. Micron. The carp was taken from the Special Swim with the bait against the sunken tree, where, a couple of nights later, I hooked and subdued a common of 16lb. 14oz. whilst sheltering from gale force winds. The weather during this October had been mild, so the carp obviously felt like feeding merrily; they were, of course, at their heaviest weight of the summer.

In early November, I had another double, a plump leather of $13^1/_2$lb., caught on sardine paste. Again the Special Swim was the location. That night the second big gale of the decade did its damnedest and I spent half the night hanging on to my brolly. The gales caused floods and damage over the country but this time it didn't scare me off the water! I did not fish Mywater again that season.

For various reasons I had fished less in the season than in the previous ten. I can't say I was sorry when March brought it to a close. I believe it was the least productive year all round for five years. The next season, in contrast, was a good one. So fickle are these carp. To those who did fish on, the going was slow and tough. The most notable fish came in the last week of the season from the Island Swim when Gary Spencer (Spen) took a fine mirror of 19lb. 12oz., on a floater.

* * *

CHAPTER 6

Worzel Gummidge and a little bit of Suicide

The close season meant netting, baiting up and some work on the water I fish regularly. The Middle Swim, with beefy syndicate members wielding pick and shovels, was made into a respectable place to fish, instead of a bankside mud patch which guaranteed dirty belongings on night sessions. Oz and I cleared away some of the hawthorns on the south bank and threw them into the edge of the Fifteen Swim (so named 'cos I caught a fifteen pounder from it), along with some larger tree branches, effectively making that swim unfishable. The reason for this bit of nonsense was because the Middle and Elliott's swims made the Fifteen Swim redundant. We planted several willows and birches against the edge of that swim and a consignment of sycamores from the garden of Pete Hall's father were planted along the south bank.

In the water, Jim Gregory and I, with my two boys and Oz carried out some gill netting to control the sprats – with, I must point out, the correct River Authority permission. On one occasion the syndicate members helped with the big seine net, but, as usual, this was less effective than the gills. The sprats were despatched and taken home for my fowl, but, towards the dawn of the new season, I decided to mix the minced flesh into 'fish fingers', dyed blue and about half the length of a normal fish finger (as advertised on T.V.!). Some of these boiled baits, other specials and some particles were boiled, dyed, scented and thrown to the wolves or consigned to the other freezer. By the time I was ready for that first trip I had in my box an assortment of shapes, smells and sizes.

One of the snags of being unable to smell is that if I use more than one bait, I have to remember the texture of shape or mark the container they are in. Serves me right for taking more than a single bait, I suppose, but I like ringing the changes when the sprats are clearing up everything going. Unless one bait is really working well I have always given myself a choice – often several. The fish fingers were not hard to spot, though; there is something decidedly unmistakable about a bait from which a solitary dead fish's eyeball peers. That and the bones sticking in sensitive fingers. It was a positively ghastly bait.

The evening of the 15th was drizzly as we set up our tackle, chatted about the prospects and who was going to catch the first thirty. The wind which scattered the droplets of water against our coats was not, thankfully, cold.

I was in Elliott's Swim, Oz had claimed the Special and Ian set up on the

Oz and his start of season doubles.

Island, and after three months' waiting the last few hours were just too much to bear so we voted to cast in early – at 7.00 p.m. Naughty, naughty.

I hooked the first fish before the first fish finger hit the bottom on the initial cast; something took the sinking bait with a wrench of the rod, then fell off! I put that down to a pike and re-cast. At 8.45 a sizzling run resulted in a hooked fish which allowed itself to be bullied out of the reed alleyway of the Gap before putting up a fight. After a short tussle I landed the fish, a mirror of 18lb. 11oz. What a satisfactory start! Half an hour later I hooked another fish, which scrapped better than the first, but weighed a little less, at 17lb. 9oz. The fish fingers were going better than well. Oz feeding maggots onto the gravelly slope of the Special Swim, was rewarded with fish of 13lb. and 16lb. His two fish also came before 10.00 p.m.

After 10.00 p.m. it poured and no more bites were forthcoming until 3.00 a.m. when the rain kindly stopped its downward rush. I cast in again and, having seen two or three carp move near to the rod tops, I dropped a mackeral special there, into nine feet of water. This bait was soon knocked or eaten off, so I re-baited and a few minutes later hooked a fish which didn't fight at all for a while. I was beginning to think it was an eel until a carp showed on the top, then commenced to fight like one, but only for a short time. Netted and weighed, that one went just under 13lb.

Whilst I was putting it in the sack, I had a run on a rod cast into the Gap. Rushing back, I reeled in and struck but the line was already through the reeds and I reluctantly had to pull the line until it broke.

The sack finally in the water, I sat down to re-hook the line I had just broken, when another bite registered. Nothing was felt on the strike, but reeling swiftly showed the fish had run towards me. I reeled in faster but the hook did not take a proper hold and within seconds, the fish was free.

The rain once again descended, but when it eased, at 4.45 a.m., I hooked a fish in the Gap on another fish finger. Whilst playing it, a churner of a run developed on the rod cast to the left, near the Rectangle opening! Before I had made up my mind what to do, that run stopped so I continued playing the fish hooked, which turned out to be a gigantic leather of at least 8lb!

Thunder and lightning were in evidence in the distance but only the rain spoilt the perfectness of those hours, though even this, when warm, gives something to a session of fishing.

The last fish I hooked that morning was played for a couple of minutes before everything went sickeningly limp. Cursing, I reeled in to see a carp's

Worzel Gummidge wouldn't get a look in.

visiting card pinned to the hook – a large scale. Landing a foul-hooked carp in Mywater is so rare as to be almost as creditable as landing one hooked in the right place! As the carp are often able to reach safety when hooked in the **mouth** they have an easier time of it when fouled in the side or tail region and so able to fight harder.

Despite having utilised a large polythene sack to keep off the majority of the rain (Worzel Gummidge wouldn't get a look in), I was very damp, so I gave the carp a little longer then went home to change into dry clothing.

The reader, whether he has fished for carp or not, can imagine my happy state of mind at the outcome of the first few hours' fishing. With a new concoction being so readily accepted and several fish on the bank, it is no wonder I was on cloud nine. The lost fish did something to dampen the joy of landed ones, but Mywater anglers have to be philosophical about such events.

Upon my return, two hours later, I cast in and almost immediately had a run on the rod to the left. The hooked fish felt big, but became entangled with a bed of hornwort and shed the hook. I hooked nothing else after that, but Oz, still entrenched in the Special, had another two carp, weighing 10lb. and 17lb. It must have been hard on poor, fishless Ian, stuck on the Island whilst Oz and I had seven doubles between us.

I had a small fish of about four pounds during the next twenty four hours, and Ian had nothing, then we packed up and went back to civilisation.

For people who hook a fair number of fish there are periods when losses get out of hand. It is as though all the little gremlins which would normally plaster things up in a relatively even manner, spread over the whole season, gang up and break your heart in a short, bitter period. I lost some fish on subsequent trips which made me wonder what I had to do to improve matters. It is strange that the season before, I had been grinding my molars because I couldn't hook the darn fish!

Arriving around 11.00 a.m. on the 21st., I had a chat with Kev who informed me he had had three fish to 15lb. in the last two days; the fifteen, he said, had spat out a few particles which he thought were maple peas. I thought otherwise, considering the Gunga beans I had thrown in at the start of the season.

At 3.00 p.m., fishing Elliott's Swim, I hooked a carp on one of my dwindling supply of fish fingers, but the fight was cut short when the hook broke at the barb. Five minute later I missed a 'perfect' take on Kit-e-Kat. Shortly after 4.00 p.m., a bait cast into the Gap was taken but the line broke, for no obvious reason, as I was pumping the carp towards me. Just before dark, I was into yet another fish, which I played in safely until the hook broke, again at the barb. I sorted out every hook from that batch and threw them angrily into the lake. Large, strong hooks they were, probably the most popular carp hook on the market, then and now. Come back Speed barbs, all is forgiven!

I had been throwing in Gunga beans since the start of the season in one place – near to the mouth of the Rectangle and almost in front of the Middle Swim. During the hours of darkness, my confidence with the bait in Mywater not very high, I had been fishing a special on top of the bean carpet. I had already hooked more than one carp off this patch, on the special, but nevertheless I decided that I really must keep the Gungas on through the night, though the roach really had acquired a taste for them (my fault for putting in too many). I really was determined to catch a carp or two on this bait. With a couple of beans on a number 1 hook to 12lb. line cast to the baited patch, I threw in a few more free offerings and settled down for the night.

At 2.45 a run developed on the bean rod. I hooked the fish but it went for a ramble into the nearest weedbed and shed the hook. Oz was fishing nearby and I joked to him that I had suffered lost fish this season through everything but being bitten off (the line severed by the carp's throat teeth). The next run on Gungas again resulted in a hooked fish which came towards me, then was off. You've guessed it, I found the line sheared an inch from the hook! Still those gremlins wouldn't go away; I was to hook and pull out of two more fish before normality returned. I have not, thank goodness, had a blight like it since. Normality is perhaps too strong a word, as a fish of 14lb. 14oz., which I caught some hours after pulling out of an earlier one, showed that carping is nothing if not a bundle of inconsistencies. I had gone to see Kev on the other side of the lake when my buzzer, on Elliott's Swim, sounded. I was tempting providence and the fish should have dropped the bait, but no, the reel handle was slowly revolving backwards when I reached the rod! I felt the fish through the Gap reeds and the line grated as I pumped the rod, but much to my surprise, the fish was coaxed back the way it had gone and netted safely.

Beleaguered, as usual, by the roach, I nonetheless decided, with night falling, to keep to double-bean cast to the left and with the pitch in mind had made four rests, 4 feet long, to enable me to fish two rods over the reeds and pointing at the Rectangle, instead of casting 'round the corner' or battering down the reed cover. With the pitch re-arranged to accommodate my new method of fishing, I threw in two or three handfuls of beans from the Middle Swim, then walked back to my chosen swim to cast in. Before dusk, the sprats stopped their interfering, fortunately, so I settled down, the bed chair warm and comfortable.

Drowsiness overcame me, eventually, and I dropped into a light sleep until the rasp of the buzzer box jolted me awake at 11.15 p.m.; I am very well trained to reacting quickly straight from the land of dreams; I know that unless I am extremely tired, my body is moving before my eyes are opened and this occasion was no exception, with the swift strike connecting with a powerful fish which seemed intent on pulling me in. The fight was so fast and exhilarating, I became convinced the fish was foul-hooked as it tore around in the deep water for five minutes or more – a long fight by Mywater standards. The carp had to surrender eventually though, and I cheered silently as I pulled him over the waiting net.

I had landed a long, slim common and I fell over everything as I hastily took net, fish and rod onto the path behind the swim. 18lb. 14oz., it went, hooked fair and square in the mouth and my biggest ever still water common carp. Some anglers never use a torch when night fishing but I do, as apart from its obvious uses, I like to have a good look at what I land in the night, as long as I am clear of the water's edge. In the beam of the Ever-Readys, I drank in the sight of that unmarked, golden fish, so fresh from its environment. The fins stood erect, as if in defiance; the mouth worked rapidly yet silently, as though the fish were giving me a telling-off from behind thick, plate glass. I sacked him down in the Mud Swim and slowly tidied up my swim.

About 3.00 a.m., I landed another common – it weighed all of four pounds. After that fish I slept again, knowing that the baits were being taken off the hooks by roach, but too tired to care. One of the syndicate members came along in the morning and took some photographs of me and my common before I slipped him gently back into the water. I went home at 11.00 a.m.

18lb 14oz: Gunga-ho!

These days, with superstar carp anglers pulling out innumerable twenty pound fish, maybe one under nineteen pounds would be deemed hardly worth a mention in the scheme of things, but I was delighted with my capture and also thankful that I am not yet at the stage in my angling career where a fish under twenty is treated with contempt. I suppose one's views on such matter are commensurate with the total of twenties one has been fortunate enough to land and whereas I have had just over a score, in sixteen years carping, there are those who have had that many in a season. Ridiculous! And sad too, because I know of more than one angler who has got himself in this position and lost much of the joy carp fishing brings. I suppose a parallel is being incarcerated with, and besieged by, hundreds of wanton females until there is little interest left. (I do not speak from experience, I am sad to report).

Sometimes I fish too long and too hard. The tiredness seems to build up, the adrenalin used in the exciting periods appears to take something out of me; makes the eyelids heavier than lead. Common sense should call "Halt! Take a kip in your proper bed for a change; dropping off to sleep at the wheel of a car doing 60 m.p.h., won't do the fishing any good!" Unfortunately, that kind of sense doesn't get through my skull very often. If the guilty feelings about neglected work and family don't step in the way, then I am off, tired or no, down the road to the silent (or otherwise!) carp lake. The buzzers will always wake me up, after all. Oh, really!

I arrived back at Mywater at 5.00 p.m., my tackle still in place where I had left it, and cast a couple of baits into the Gap. Then went into a coma for a couple of hours. Awakening, I discovered the right-hand bait had been taken and the line was snagged in the Gap reeds. The inevitable breakage occurred, finally, and I swore (not for the first time), at my stupidity in letting a fish run around the pit with, perhaps, yards of line trailing behind it.

At 8.30 I had what must have been the millionth walk round the perimeter of the lake and looking from the lane into the New Swim, I saw a fish struggling weakly in the hornwort. Closer inspection, from the water's edge, revealed the fish to be a carp of about 13 pounds, attached to a fishing line, which in turn, was anchored to the weeds. Presumably this was the fish I had broken on over an hour before. Shamefacedly, I used a dead tree branch to snag the line and draw it to the bank. I handlined the carp right to my feet before it succeeded in breaking the line near the hook and swimming off.

Back at my pitch, I put out the baits for the night and settled down to a perpetual movement of the Gunga bean baits – roach. In the early hours, the special, which had lain untouched in the Gap, was taken and I found myself fighting a lively enough fish which proved to be a fat mirror of 12lb 13oz. I finally did take a rest after that – going home for a couple of days to catch up on sleep and family life.

On the Tuesday (27th), I rolled up at Mywater and had a look round. Spen and Andy, two ever-cheerful syndicate members, on their first full season as the water, not too cheerfully reported a couple of fish hooked and lost by themselves and one syndicate member had landed a twenty.

Again in Elliott's Swim, I fished the night, with the water temperature at 58° F., but had no luck and left for work at 6.30 a.m., leaving the gear where it was. I was back down again after a day's 'work', only detouring to my home to collect baits and food.

Casting out, I sat back to eat a sandwich or two and drink a cup of tea. After an hour, I reeled in, selected a rod, my net and bait and went for a wander to the far bank where I found some fish.

In the Little Tree Swim, I struck at a biting carp, pulling the bait out of its mouth. Moving a few paces to the Swamp, I was a little too eager to see what was lying in there and scared a couple of decent fish. Oh, what a gay day!

Deciding that carp fishing just wasn't my forte, I cleared out a few reeds and dead branches. It is amazing how dead branches grow like the clappers in my lake, you know. Must be the only water in the country where the spontaneous generation of dead branches occurs.

The New Swim was next on my list. I thought that I could give that swim a whirl then all the carp in the lake would be scared to death and hiding in No. 1 Swim, where I would move my tackle and fish the night. I didn't manage to scare 'em though; I must have been stricken with an attack of invisibility because several carp near the bank continued cruising around with no apparent fear.

Joking apart, the movements whilst fishing for these creatures at close range have to be slow and all attendant cover has to be utilised. It is surprising how much effort is used whilst creeping in slow motion to a certain vantage point and I was warm by the time my sweetcorn bait was dangling from a patch of surface weed.

Two or three carp in the vicinity of the bait, studiously ignored it as they promenaded, so I decided to lower the bait in the edge amongst a handful of sweetcorn I dropped in. The creamy film of juice from the bait clouded the water and after I had lowered the hook bait, two carp swam along and stopped on entering the smelly area. It is not often you get the chance to witness such a happening, but there was no doubt in my mind that those fish pulled up on smelling the scented water. One of the carp seemed as if it was about to put its head down, but then changed its mind and swam off. The second fish sank to the vertical and began mopping up the loose feed. I watched my hook bait, then he began to move away and I considered that that was my lot – but the line was going out! I had been looking at the wrong bits of corn!

The strike was a formality and the fish fought well, but the bush to the left and the bank snags to the right offered no immediate danger; the biggest problem was that I didn't have a handle to my landing net! I can't for the life of me think why not and it isn't recorded in my little blue book, but I do know I am for ever ruining net handles. I had to play the fish for much longer than normal, until it was really tired. It was not large, by any means, but worth the wet foot I collected in getting the handleless net under him and hauling fish and net up the bank. A 13lb 9oz. mirror.

The night again passed eventless and once more I had to finish early to go to work.

On the Friday, I again visited Mywater, and Jay came along too. After the usual sniff around, I set up shop in the Special Swim then had a look into the New Swim, and put a handful of corn on the clear patch whence the last fish had been taken. No sooner had the yellow stuff landed gently on the silt, than a long, dark fish began sniffing around, moved to the bait and ate a few grains, then slowly drifted away. Jay quietly brought a rod, then crept a few yards back to fetch the landing net. I hooked on a couple of grains and lowered them to the small area the free baits covered.

It wasn't long before the carp was back, this time with a mirror of around twelve pounds and a couple of small commons. Luckily, only the largest of the group seemed interested, but first he stirred the silt around, picking up the loose bits of corn one by one from the roots of the grass, 3 feet down. Slowly the fish worked its way along, taking its time; like a gourmet savouring every mouthful of a fine meal. Even closer it came and I twitched the line, stirring the bait a fraction, just to ensure I was looking at the right spot this time.

The few baits left near the ones with a steel centre, were sucked in, then a small common came to the carp and nudged its bigger brother as if in warning. Fortunately, this action was ignored and I watched the hook bait

Leather double.

shoot into the mouth of the fish. This is the best of carp fishing; standing out crouching directly over a big fish, watching its every move, every flicker of the fins, seeing the mud swirling, the weeds gently waving; observing the extended mouth working over a small area of the lake bed, picking items so delicately from their resting places. It is a pity, when we are lucky enough to be so close to nature, that we end all normal action with violence. The strike was made, with my rod tip directly over his head and he thrashed the water in the one spot, bending the rod right round. He just did not know where to go or what to do. After a few seconds, with a very small amount of line taken off the reel, the carp continued to thrash and I took the net off Jay (complete with handle), lowered it into the water slowly and edged the carp over it, all in one (graceful) movement. As simple as that.

Oz turned up just as we were lifting the fish from the water: 16lb. 10oz. of mirror looked fine in the evening light. It was my 8th double from Mywater in just over two weeks; how silly the previous year was beginning to look. There is just no understanding carp fishing sometimes.

Night fishing was doing me no good at all, it seemed, because again, I caught nothing. The only interesting event was carp sucking and knocking at the home-made, green-dyed crust I had thrown in before dark. Until this time, I had always scoffed at the serious use of crust (floater) in Mywater, because the carp gave little sign that they were interested in anything that floated on top of the water. With proof that carp were taking a positive interest in floating baits, I vowed to throw the stuff in on a more regular basis and observe reactions.

After the dawn came and went, it was a dull, dry day. With Jay happily catching sprats off the Island, I read and wandered around until 2.00 p.m., before calling it a day and going home.

* * *

The obsessional, fifty-two weeks a year religion must wear away at the nerves of Susan, the long, long sufferer of my addiction. If the carp man is not fishing, then he is talking about carp; when he is fishing he is still talking about carp. On and on. Carp, carp, carp. How? Why? How big are they? How small are they? Can I get a ticket? Can I poach? Does that smell O.K.? If only I had been there that day instead of at work. Petrol, food, sandwiches, soups, baits; multitudes of baits – the freezer's full of them. Rods in the kitchen want bagging, reels in the living room need

Genuine leather!

wiping. Magazines in the bedroom, blankets in the garage. Grind on. Talk, chat, cry, swear, curse, laugh. Torment, happiness, tiredness. Hello kids. Goodbye kids. I'm sorry kids. God, it really scrapped .... landed it and was as sick as a parrot. Kitchen pans stink of curry; kitchen stinks of curry a la dogmeat. Cat's had it. Baby's had it and wiped it all over her new romper suit. Show you how this method works; fill the bath to the top – see how the Alka Seltzer dissolves so quickly? Natter, natter. Rabbit, rabbit. Telephone calls. Letters from Rod. Tea on the sofa with Nige, Oz. Don't know anyone except anglers. Hell of a socialiser, aren't I? Just one more trip will do it – they just have to feed after all this time. Not saying a word about the bait – not to anybody. Asleep when the buzzer went, dreaming of a carp taking the bait and the buzzer going.... I'll go after the film has finished – well, perhaps a bit later, nudge, nudge. Just a few more ounces and it would have gone doubles. Wind's south-west, good, that'll shift 'em.

I love every second of it.

* * *

A few days later, after putting two tinfulls of broad beans into the Special Swim over a couple of days, I eventually had a run on single bean and landed a 14lb. 12oz. common, using 15lb. bs. Micron dyed with Meltonian Leather Dye (you rub on a few coats). There was nothing special about the common or its capture, but once again my tendency to change baits at the drop of a hat showed up. Strangely enough, although I always fish the 'going' bait on at least one of my rigs, it is often the experimental bait which is taken.

The next fish just scraped double figures – a 10lb. 3oz. mirror which came from Elliott's Swim on part of a boiled sausage, cast on to the side of the New Swim ridge, where the reeds are thin. The subsequent mirror of 15lb. 13oz. was tempted with mackerel paste cast to the same spot, but from the Island. Everything was going fine. That last fish was landed with the hook just past the gill cover, but a fresh and bleeding hole well inside the mouth proved that it had first been hooked in the 'you can claim that one region'. The journey the mirror had made into a weedbed before being landed accounted for the changing of the hook position.

Another interesting point; very, very rarely in Mywater have carp been landed with spare tackle affixed to them, although some are certainly hooked and lost more than once in a season. The carp appear to shed hooks with ease

A T24 + 15lb micron = 18lb 8oz carp.

once the line has broken (and sometimes when it hasn't!).

The water temperature, since the season had began, rarely had risen above 60° F. and I had not been swimming at all. Mind you, I had been hooking so many carp there had been little time for acting porpoise.

On the 12th July, I took another small leather, this time from the New Swim. I had hooked the small double with a bait cast to the right in nine feet of water, near the bank-side snags. I am not too fond of fishing the New Swim because the average fish landed seems to be small and quite a lot – probably the larger ones – have been lost in the snags. Despite this, I fished the New Swim again, a few days later and still cast one of the baits to the right.

The voles, as usual, scurried around under the bramble bushes that night, intent on their business, which, if I wasn't too careful, included filching my baits or feed. The mosquitoes seemed around for ever, trying to get through the canopy of the net-curtaining bag I put on my face to thwart their attention. An owl uttered its screeching call from the direction of the big willow; the voles, though, rattling, clattering, chattering as ever, did not halt their progress, perhaps secure in the knowledge that the predator would not dare to venture where a human lay.

At 12.15, the night dark and warm, the line began to move on the right-hand rod and I found myself into a fish which moved away from the snags and swam around the centre of the swim at a terrific pace. With a T24 rod and 15lb. bs. Micron, I did not fear the tackle would let me down and an 18lb 8oz. mirror came to the net. To combat the sprats, the bait had been a rock-hard special, flavoured with some substance or other. I thought it rather fitting that a carp which could imitate an express train should munch a special which had been doing a good impression of a cannon ball.

A couple of weeks and two blank trips passed by before I landed another fish from Mywater. This was taken from the Moped on a green-dyed crust and weighed 13lb. 4oz. I lost a couple of fish over the next few days; one, taking chocolate paste, fell off when the hook pulled out and one on Bounce special took the bait down so far it chewed through the line with its throat teeth.

Third time lucky. In the New Swim, I hooked a fish on Bounce special and after a short tussle, landed a common of 15lb. exactly.

The relative ease with which I was hooking carp was making a mockery of the previous season. No appreciable change in tackle or tactics had been made, yet the last fish had been my fifteenth double from the lake – a record, according to Nigel.

The problems of hooking fish in the Swamp and the Little Tree Swim had manifested themselves during recent sessions. In the Swamp, particularly, there were times when I was at a loss; if I watched the bait when an interested carp came into the swim, it (the carp) would blow up a cloud of silt, obscuring what was happening. On the other hand, watching the line or an indicator to register a bite usually resulted in a strike at the wrong time, thus scaring the fish off. Sometimes baits were taken off the hook with little or no indication of a bite. As soon as the problems became obvious, they faded away again, for the time being, at least.

In the next month, I decided to improve prospects in Fred's Hole, situated in the Rectangle reedbeds. Previously I had usually cast to the thinned-out patch from the conventional position, but due to my lousy casting ability, I didn't think much of this state of affairs. There was some potential in making the suicide spot more of a pitch and less of a liability, so I undertook the job.

Some bright spark had made a gap through the bankside thorns directly in front of the point of interest, so that the fish could see any entrance an angler made, especially as the brightest part of the sky was a backlight, the bank being the southern one. I filled in the existing opening with dead branches and made another, a little further to the west, cutting out the prickly branches and slanting in to the reeds, on the bank and in the water, until it was possible to fish two rods into the right spot without ripping an artery open getting in, or, once there, cutting the rods in half on the stalks of the reeds.

A large piece of board was dragged round from the north bank, pulled in to the new, improved swim, and deposited on the boggy part of the bank as a platform, should I want to fish the spot without wellies. Operations were now complete and I washed my hands, satisfied I had done what I could to improve the chances of hooking and landing carp from the spot.

A fortnight later, I began fishing the water again, and except for having to clear out some broken reeds, the swim was fine. The carp must have thought it was fine too, because I reverted to the habit of throwing in a handful of luncheon meat cubes, every now and then, and they were all being eaten.

Half an hour in the Suicide Spot resulted in a quick bite which I couldn't hit before the bait was dropped. When two further handfuls of luncheon meat had gone from the muddy patch in the reeds, during the next hour or so, I again took my rod and quietly lowered in a bit, placing the rod on the rests already in position. The leger this time, was directly on the line on a 1oz. bomb stopped a couple of inches from the hook. I had a good bite soon after lowering the bait into the water, but attention to my bait container caused me to miss that bite too.

Over a period of time, yet more cubes were taken from the reeds. Trying for a third time to hook a carp, I used two rods. I lowered in the left bait, which sank a few feet beyond the rod tip, then the right bait was put in the water and I was attaching the silver paper indicator to the line when the first one began to move slowly up to the butt ring. I bent into the fish, as surprised as he, no doubt, and sweated a little as it thrashed under the rod tip before I could grasp the net and shove it under the fish. My prize was Blunt Nose, our friendly common at 16lb. 12oz.

Although I didn't realise it at the time, I had invented the 'bolt rig', which is the careful positioning of a heavy lead near to the hook with the intention of making the carp bolt with the bait in its mouth, giving a good bite indication. Of course, my intentions had nothing to do with making carp bolt, but there we are. It just goes to show what a talented inventor I am. Unwittingly I have probably conjured up what could be some of the most useful inventions known to humanity; it is just a case of forgetting what they were **supposed** to be and working out what their true application **could** be. Now I did make some slow-sinking legers, perhaps their potential in the field of astro physics should be investigated....

The day after catching Blunty, I visited Mywater directly from work with one thought: to fish the Suicide Spot.

My two baits were cast in by 5.10 p.m. and I settled down to wait. It is great fun in these reedbed swims because when the wind is not too strong, one can watch the reed stems wavering as fish brush past them – and a lot of the time the fish are carp – and often they are knocking a reed next to which lies a baited hook! I hadn't waited long before the nearest loop of silver paper trembled and began to move, causing the instinctive reaction of a strike.

The fish, in its thrashing fury, tangled the line in the reeds but I was able to free it as the water was frothed and with little ceremony, the net was whipped under the fish and I was back on the grassy path behind the swim, the whole action taking seconds rather than minutes. Laying the carp on the grass behind the swim, I rooted round for my scales, finally hoisting the carp up in my sack to weigh in at 16lb. 6oz.

*My prize was Blunt Nose,
our friendly common, at 16lb 10oz.*

After admiring the fish for a little while, I slipped it back via the Middle Swim and went home, arriving there at 6.30, my mission for the day accomplished in short order.

The final few trips to Mywater that summer, (which God kindly extended almost to the end of October), saw a pair of fish lost and three more doubles up to 14lb. 1oz., landed, all taking luncheon meat. The season had turned out to be my best ever at the water, with a record twenty doubles. Strangely, considering what had gone before, none of the fish had weighed over twenty pounds. I was not complaining though.

I did no fishing at all at Mywater during the winter.

* * *

CHAPTER 7

An Ocean of Blackberries

I fished for only two nights at Mywater during the opening fortnight of the new season. The carp fed with gusto those two weeks and the syndicate members did well, taking two twenty pound fish and over a dozen doubles. The carp must have known I was not around again.

My two trips saw me lose a fish in the Rectangle suicide spot, land a monster of 4lb., and lose a further one on butterscotch-flavoured pellets from the Middle Swim.

This season, surface baits really came back with a bang (or at least a slurp). After years when the baits were virtually ignored, the carp were sitting up and taking notice.

The fish I hooked in the Rectangle took hot dog sausage, a bait I had been very backward in coming forward with at Mywater, but which, next to Kit-e-Kat and luncheon meat, was to prove the best single bait I have used there. Trying hard as I have been not to lose the chronological order of this epic in a welter of time-shuttling (going back and forth, chum), I will let the facts speak for themselves.

Just about 10.00 a.m., on the sunny 1st July, Jay and I arrived at Mywater. Number one son opted to fish for sprats off the Middle Swim, whilst I wandered about like a vagrant with itchy pants.

I had finally decided that the best way to fish the Swamp, the Rectangle suicide spot and a few other places close to the bank, was to put a swan shot 1"–2" from the hook, ascertain the depth with a small float and strike as soon as the float lifted. Nothing new in this idea, of course, although the application has a certain novelty. Floats are not used a lot in carp fishing, the main reason being, I suppose, because we usually use two or three rods so a float on one or more tends to cause more problems than it solves. We could well catch more, in many circumstances, if we used one float rod and nothing else, but the concentration needed to watch an unmoving float for hours on end is too much, for me at least. I am quite convinced, by the way, that float tackle does not scare carp half as much as it scares the majority of carp anglers.

Ten minutes in the Suicide Spot produced a lift on the float and the instant strike was enough to hook a fish which did not do anything except almost lose its head from its shoulders. When I had finished scowling ruefully at the smallest carp I had landed for years, I slipped the 4lb common back.

For a time I fished the Middle Swim alongside Jay, very cleverly avoiding my eyes being pulled out by his repeated casting of a size 18 on which, sharing the fate of Spartacus and Jesus, was a crucified maggot, destined to a slow and torturous end. I had ten minutes in the Swamp and sat in the Secret Place, watching one or two small doubles wandering about almost as aimlessly as I had been doing. The whole world was passing by slowly, the air still enough to allow my cigar smoke to drift upwards in a straight column of shaded grey; only the plopping of Jay's tackle hitting the water across the way broke the quietness of those moments.

Later in the afternoon, I looked again in the Swamp to see a couple of good fish there. My rod was on the other side of the lake! I hurried back, sweating profusely, and grabbed my standard close-work gear for the snaggy swims at $1^1/_2$lbs test curve Jack Hilton compound taper rod, 15lb test braided Micron, 410 reel and a thick-wire salmon hook.

Back to the pitch I pushed in a rest alongside the bank reeds and put the float on the half inch length of valve rubber which was already on the line. I adjusted the float, then lowered the section of hot dog sausage into the water, the swan shot on the line near the hook taking the bait down quickly. The butt end of the rod was propped on a convenient broken branch. The carp I had spotted a little while earlier had gone on to pastures new, but I was determined to stay until something came along.

Determination was needless, for within a few short minutes, as I stood peering over the vegetation, a good fish slowly moved into the restricted area of the Swamp and ambled around. The bait was well away from the fish and I watched in anguish for minutes that seemed hours as the quarry blew bubbles and silt in various directions, seemingly unaware that a nice titbit lay nearby. Eventually, the scent of the sausage meat must have been irresistible for our friend because it went towards the bait, stirring a cloud of silt round its head as it reached the target. The rod now in my hand, I watched the float intently, saw it jerk, then lay flat. I struck and the fish was on. The reel clutch was screwed right down and a finger on the spool made doubly sure no line could be taken as the carp beat the water to a froth. Everything held, luckily, and the fish could only swim with ever decreasing energy until it was exhausted; I pushed the net out and under. Mine!

Float and hook were both loose in the net as I laid the fish on the bank. Jay, who had scooted round upon my shout of, "I'm in," said breathlessly that he had seen a twenty before and this was another! I was more modest with my estimate, thinking it about 18 pounds. The scales showed Jay to be right; 20lb 12oz the fish weighed. I was not just pleased with capturing another

The scales showed Jay to be right;
20lb 12oz the fish weighed.

twenty, but also with the fact that it had come from such a difficult area – the swim had not, in fact, produced a twenty before.

Like so many captures of good fish, the aftermath is often an anti-climax and so the blank night in the Middle Swim proved to be.

Until I once again went where no man had gone before, the Secret Place was untouched – a virgin spot on the perimeter of Mywater. In the latter weeks of the close season, I had bashed a way through the massed brambles from the New Swim and watched the carp I knew were always around the bottom of the Gap. I christened it the Secret Place because it was! I wanted it for the observation of carp, not the casting of hooks, or the treading of careless, clumsy feet, so I never entered it when anyone else was on the water, and when its accessibility **was** discovered, I let it be known that anyone caught in that spot would be out of the syndicate; I desired to try out free offerings where I was sure they would be looked upon as food and not a trick with a hook in it and, ultimately, the bottom of the Gap, fished from this spot, seemed the likeliest place to tempt the biggest carp in the lake.

* * *

...Well, another day, another dollar. Wonder how my luck will fall? Wrong side of good, no doubt. Sky's a shade cloudy – weather men speak of rain so there's a chance it will be 90° in the shade and we'll all die of sun-stroke. The way I feel at the moment, a nice slow death would do me the world of good. Ha! Morbid so and so today, isn't the ole boy?; that bottom lip will soon grow so heavy he'll topple over on his face. If you had my problems, sir, you'd be fed up. You've got the angels to play with whereas I've not, which is part of the reason I'm down, I suppose. I've not had a good sleep for weeks, everything seems to be piling up and to top it all I've got to go to work all this week in pain of getting the sack. Life isn't worth much at the moment. It's not as though I had murdered someone. Fair enough, had I committed murder I could understand everything getting me down; sort of a punishment before the trial, you might say. What's the use of complaining though? On the brighter side, I'll probably tackle up and hook a big one first throw. Come to think of it, I'm going to fish the Special so I'd only lose the bloody fish in the tree. There are ways and ways of escaping a bit of mental turmoil. Could always cut off the odd ear or two to show the world (and his wife) what I feel inside my chest. I

don't like beer, wine and spirits so becoming drunk is out. Don't take drugs either, so getting high on a black banana or whatever they call 'em is just not on. I don't know how to buy drugs, anyhow. Are you supposed to hang around public toilets to get drugs? No, that's how you get arrested. The best thing to do is to take the car back up the lane and motor round the county a little – fast. Driving like a fool when depressed has the effect on me, of sending the adrenalin round my tubes and taking me out of my previous mood. Let's face it, when you're doing 80 round a tight bend you're too busy messing yourself to bother about the worries that put you in that position in the first place. Yes, I think I'll go and have a burn. One question; where's the money for the petrol coming from? That's a point – the tank is nearly empty and I've only got enough money on me to buy a pack of cigars. So much for a burn. Damn. (Peer myopically over the bushes into the New Swim). Crackerjack! Size of that one! It seems as though it is looking for food, too; could be a good session after all. Now have I got the Hilti set up in the car with the 11lbs Maxima on it...

* * *

One morning, just before leaving at the end of a fruitless night session filled with 'bites' I couldn't hit, I threw into the Secret Place, the seven specials I had remaining. To my surprise, five floated, so I sat for a while to see if any interest would be shown by carp.

I had, on the suggestion of my wife, been rolling and boiling specials in the normal way, then soaking them in water to which had been added the flavour I wanted to impart on the baits, rather than putting in the smell before the boiling process. This ensured that the nature of the pong was not destroyed and also guaranteed that the smell was on the outside and not 'locked in'. Without a doubt the aroma escapes from boiled specials but due to some problems I had been having during this period, with my baits, I had adopted Susan's suggestion: it is a rather messy way of going about the job of enticing carp though.

I have already made quite clear my intention of keeping away from the 'serious' bits regarding carp fishing, in respect of baits and methods, and I am sure I have succeeded in this aim, wanting to entertain rather than inform. Sticking to the simple life with baits at Mywater, rather than using a degree of sophistication has probably cost me fish, but with colour, smell and shape

Banks

P. Banks

P. Banks.

being the three important factors of a good bait, I am sure there is still plenty of scope left for me without going over the top. Besides, due to my large family and the fact that my work is sadly neglected because of the fishing, I have not always had a great deal of money to spare for some of the concoctions which are reputed to work wonders on other waters. What does work wonders on Mywater is stealth of feet, keen, watching eyes and the willingness to raise oneself off one's bum and go looking.

Back to the floating specials.

Five or six doubles to 18 pounds or so slopped about on the surface near the baits, the largest fish playing water polo with the floaters. It was a heartening sight to see the fish so uncaring of danger after all the hooks they have had thrown at them and I considered how daft it would be to blow the swim by fishing it.

A few days later, a westerly was blowing into the Moped Swim, on a sunny evening and almost inevitably carp were in the east end. As I scurried up the spotting tree to the side of the swim, at least a dozen doubles were scattered around the Moped and the Dead End, at various angles to the bank.

I fired out some butterscotch floater upwind of the fish and flicked a few pieces into the Dead End where a fish soon showed interest by nosing about on the surface scum collected against the reeds. My rods were ready in the car so it was but a minute's work to set up the net, which Jay carried for me, and position myself in a gap twixt the bushes overlooking the very bottom of the lake.

One carp in particular was interested in the surface debris, as it sucked in leaves, dust and bits of bait, spitting most out but retaining a couple of the pieces of floater, so I cast a bait well out of the way of the fish and gently drew it back to lodge against some surface weeds in a position I hoped the carp would visit. As if in a teasing mood, the double went away, but obviously relenting, came back a few minutes later and slurped at the surface rubbish near to the bait.

Slowly he neared the bait and suddenly the floater was gone and the hook was into a hard fighting fish. Up and down the Dead End he went and I hung on to the rod with my right hand whilst trying to disentangle the landing net Jay had thoughtfully wrapped round the nearest bramble bush!

I was using 11.5lb, bs. Platil Strong and that fish tested it to the limit until I freed the damned net and slipped it into the water. As if this was a signal, the fish decided it had had enough and allowed me to draw it gently between the arms. I had been at the water for only a few minutes and a fine, fat leather of 15lb 9oz was already mine.

The night, as so often at Mywater, was blank with just a few pulls on my baits. In the morning I fed the carp in my Secret Place with flavoured trout pellet specials. I was able, even, to take some photographs of Blunt Nose, the camera hogger, taking floater off the top. Seeing large fish mopping up baits as if there was no tomorrow, tickled me, after all the times I had left a bait in a swim for hours on end without so much as a decent lift of the indicators.

The next few weeks proved paradoxical; flavoured baits such as lemon, orange and almond were eaten with great gusto in the Secret Place, yet produced no hook fish elsewhere. This lack of reward with the baits made me scratch my head, I must admit.

It was not a great year for Mywater carp, except for the initial ten days when they went mad, but odd fish were caught by the others through the summer.

* * *

They are not frightened to pinch the baits off the hook, are they? Nor slow to escape once hooked, those awkward, heartless devils. Long might I walk the banks searching, only to hook and lose the fish once found – or not to hook them at all.

The noise the reeds make as the wind stirs them seems to be a chuckle of contempt at my ineptitude; their nodding heads saying, "You're just not up to it, pal". The hawthorns and brambles still catch the net, or rod, or coat; still cause little annoyances, even though the fish they are protecting are not being harmed.

In the evening, the mosquitoes, breeding in the stagnant, swampy regions, attack by the pint pot full – battalions, armadas, squadrons of the devils. Holding a seminar on the skin, sucking blood, sating their appetite; slowly changing from shrivelled, empty husks to red and bloated bags of my blood. All the sufferings have to be endured though, carp caught or not.

* * *

At the beginning of August, I took the unusual step of landing a nice common weighing 15lbs 5oz from the Moped. Casting under the far bank, at 3.00 a.m., I had a searing run and the strike proved that something was hanging on, which was wriggling very little. I reeled straight in and netted the 'fish', then realised that I had engulfed with my net a large clump of hornwort. The next netful of the weed had the common inside it. Carp, when hooked amidst a bundle of weeds, often do not fight. A typical 'ostrich with its head in the sand' situation. Hornwort, being virtually rootless, is not a bad weed to wrap up a carp in, if you want to land it without a scrap. Mind you, thick weed beds are not to be treated lightly.

Next I hooked a small double in the Moped Swim which, before the hook broke at the barb, did a spot of ballet dancing on the surface, the like of which would have given Dame Margot heartburn. As soon as it was lost, I cast out again and had a take whilst placing the indicator on the line. The bait was dropped before I could pick up the rod. Some time later, I hooked yet another fish, but this time reeled in a scale.

Finally, at mid-day, I hooked a fourth fish which managed (it seemed) to entangle the line in every patch of weed and all the sunken branches in Mywater, so I had to strip off and paddle in up to my neck to land it. If I were 5' 2" tall instead of 6' 2" I wouldn't have landed half the carp I **have** caught in my time; I would long ago have met a watery end. The fish, a leather of 14lb 5oz didn't really console me after the day's events, so I dried off and went home.

For two weeks I fished elsewhere before visiting Mywater again on September 7th. Nige and Oz had been to the water in the week and had hooked seven carp between them, mainly on Go Cat hoops, which the carp were going mad over, it seemed. Oz's three fish had all, sadly fallen off, but Nige's four all were landed and all were doubles to fifteen pounds. Not being one to resist the chance of a drop of fun, I arrived at 8.00 a.m., on the first available day, looked round and saw little, so tackled up in the Special after firing hoops into several likely looking areas.

The bottom bait I put in was a section of hot-dog sausage and one of the surface baits was the same, supported by the dead and floating reeds in the far left-hand corner of the swim. Go Cat, on the third rod, was lobbed on the surface hornwort against the sunken tree.

I knew that a bait which sinks in water can be used effectively as a floater when lying on surface weed and the sausage was in an area I was sure the carp would patrol, so I wasn't surprised when that bait was taken and I was into a hooked fish. The carp fought well but my Special Swim gear of terylene line and soft rod sapped its strength and after trying desperately to dive into the tree, it soon gave up and was netted, proving to be a plump leather of 16lb 12oz. Lovely!

After the crashing and thumping in the Special I decided to move and fish, for the first time, my Secret Place. Despite waiting and observing for almost three months, I had not seen a really big fish there and although I had been having a poor time at the water during the season, I had resisted the temptation to fish the spot. Watching the carp had been fun enough, but now, with the nights beginning to draw in, and my fishing likely to be cut at any time by the need to make habitable a run-down cottage I had purchased, I considered the time was right to have a go.

Well, that has taken care of the excuses; I am next found sitting on a broken tree branch in the Secret Place, surrounded by an ocean of blackberry bushes, looking at three carp, all good fish, taking Go Cat hoops off the surface against the bank. The largest fish had a mark on the left gill cover and I thought it was the twenty pounder I had caught earlier that season. I dangled a couple of rings on to the surface, directly below the rod tip, near to the largest of the fish and very soon it sucked in the bait. With my luck it would **have** to be the biggest, just ask Nigel. I struck firmly, stood up and kept the fish's head high as it plunged under the rod like a wild mustang. There was no real danger, despite the snags to the left, and the fish was soon in the net.

Getting the fish to the lane was not too easy but no main arteries were sliced beyond repair by the grasping fronds. I saw that the mark on the gill cover was not a scar but a pea-sized growth, suggesting to me that I had not seen this fish before. At 19lb 6oz it was my second fifteen-plus fish of the day and the time was still only 11.15 a.m.

After sacking the latest fish, I wandered about, looking for another chance. The breeze ruffling the water's surface was variable in direction and as such was not pushing either the floaters or the carp in any particular direction, but a few carp were in the bay below the big willow, so I opted for fishing there. In the past I had fished just above water level in this area but, as I get older I seem to become a little dafter, so I clambered up the tree and sat, fifteen feet above water level, with the baits in a bag, clenched between my teeth and the rod grasped in my hands. The view, higher up, was much better and I was able to locate and estimate the size of the carp near to, or on the top. Some were gliding in and out of the hornwort beds; others were moving alongside the corner by the Twenty Swim, now and then going out of sight under the dead, floating reeds accumulated there, to re-appear further along the 'raft'. My climbing, done with the slowness (if not the grace) of a three-toed sloth had not scared the quarry, so very soon the hoops I dropped were being taken in. I lowered two hoops on to the surface and held them there, just tripping the water, which isn't easy, believe me, when the hook is trying to sink them and the breeze is shaking the line; fortunately, my nerves are pretty good, so the bait held steady enough.

As I perched uncomfortably in the tree, a leopard waiting for a victim, five carp came from the Plateau, taking baits on the surface as they swam slowly my way. One detached itself from the group and swam up to inspect my bait. I thought the fish, unmistakably Blunt Nose, wasn't going to take the bait as he inspected it very thoroughly, but suddenly the hoops were gone and I pulled the hook home. On the 11lb line, Blunty scrapped well but, despite scaring to death every other carp within three miles, he could not do much about the relentless pressure from above. I had to ensure that he was well tired so I allowed him to paddle round for longer than normal before risking my neck, my fish and, perhaps, my prospects, in the journey down the tree trunk.

No easy matter, inching down a tree trunk, with a double figure fish on the end of the line, looking to escape into the handiest weedbed; it is necessary to reel in, keeping the tension on the line whilst sliding down and also holding on to the tree. It must be quite a hilarious sight to see and any further parallels with the sloth would be rather incongruous. Eventually, breathless, hot but at water level, and still in one piece, I reached for my net and made my capture safe and sound. I was pleasantly surprised that old Blunty weighed in at his heaviest ever – a fit 17lb 2oz.

I now had to catch some sleep as I was due to go into 'work' that night for a ten hour shift, so I settled back in the Special, emerging at 5.00 p.m. from the blissful depths and soon had the carp taking hoops again. I could not hook one in the Special or the New Swim, despite trying for quite some time, so I decided to try once more in the Secret Place. I threw in some rings and waited for a few minutes before the fish came through the New Swim reeds and began feeding.

To avoid hooking the smaller fish which came in I had to pull the hook-bait off the surface several times, which is rather akin to having your dinner sink through the table top every time you go for a fork-full. At 6.15 four good fish were virtually fighting to get the free offerings down them so I lowered

Four doubles catch.

Me, a fidget and a mirror.

the baited hook, giving each a 25% chance of acquiring a sore mouth. Inevitably, one sucked in the hook – the fourth carp over 15lb that day to wind up on the bank, at 15lb 14oz.

Photographing the fish was rather a fuss and palaver and really I should not condone the retaining of carp for quite long periods by even suggesting I went for a picture of all four, but I have the negatives as evidence, so what else can I say! Fortunately, the carp came to no harm on the sacks laid on the lane grass and all were gently returned via the Moped Swim, physically none the worse for their adventures.

The following day, I landed another fish of 14lb 12oz from the Special Swim surface rubbish, but to make sure I did not become too cocky, the carp, on my next three trips, refused to attach themselves to my hooks.

A week later, my youngest boy, Boysie, had insisted on sharing a few hours of my carp fishing time, so he was with me as I moved round the water, attracting nothing, before sitting in the Secret Place and putting out a few hoops.

The blue-backs I fish for generally come through the reeds from the New Swim and spend a short time in the Gap, sometimes sinking to the bottom alongside the bank to feed on whatever is available on the bare, silt patch there. On the right, the fish come from the short, reedy channel leading to the Swamp. It seems an idyllic life, drifting from spot to spot, feeding as the mood or food supply dictates; and it is certainly idyllic to watch the carp as the sun crosses from left to right, warming soul and body. A fish on the bank is often just a bonus.

Before long, the two carp resident in the bottom of the Gap – fish of 12 or 13 pounds – began taking the odd bait. Another, larger carp came in and out of the area several times and I kept my eye on him with a view to him having an accident with a hook.

Feeding in sinking baits at the edge, when the carp had their backs turned, had the effect of attracting the fish onto the bottom to eat the food, so I had slipped into the habit of putting bait down there whenever I had sat in the swim during the previous months of being merely a spectator in the Secret Place. Now I fed in chunks of hot-dog sausage and watched the carp go down. I couldn't see the dark baits, but assumed they were being eaten.

As Boysie sat near to the entrance of the swim, hidden from the fish, finishing off his sweets and sandwiches and beginning to fidget and grumble a little, as youngsters are apt to do, I juggled the bait around in an attempt to get it into the mouth of the biggest carp. To prevent the hoops floating off the hook, I had pushed a small piece of sausage on to the point, later to be replaced by a $^1/_2$" length of a dried stalk of couch grass. Twice I struck when it seemed a fish was hookable, but both times pulled the bait out of the mouth of the startled fish. Even in this swim they were becoming cagey. The scaring effect of my actions, of course, prolonged the waiting and I got the impression Boysie was by now beginning to consider going along the bank and vandalising the odd tree.

I decided, as I had had enough of my companion's grumbling, to blow the selection and let them get on with it, so I let the bait sink to the bottom on the clear patch and waited for a bite. Soon a small carp came through the swim, followed by a bigger one. The small carp carried on swimming, the big one chose to sink to where the bait was and begin rooting about. I lost sight of the hoops, thought they were in the carp's mouth and struck. The satisfying wrench on the rod told me I had guessed right.

Lots of splashing on the surface happened, which was becoming par for the course recently and the fish swam in a circular direction, then, Boysie now close behind me, the net was in the water and the carp was scooped into it. The mirror I had landed weighed 18lb 7oz., a plumper than normal carp for Mywater. Boysie was not bored any more.

After we had taken a few pictures, I took Boysie home, then travelled back to Mywater to fish out the night. Excuse me for mentioning it, but the dark hours passed with me and, seemingly the carp, in a coma.

In contrast, the following night in the New Swim was active. The carp really had acquired the taste for hot-dog sausage, several being taken off the surface hornwort. I pulled the hook out of the first fish, the line was bitten off on the second bite and this third run produced a large rat dangling on the line, struggling violently in the air as I debated how to deal with it. Luckily the rodent gnawed through the line and saved me the anguish of having to take hold of it. At a little before six I landed an 11lb 12oz fish, with several hook wounds in its mouth. Great night!

* * *

Sandwiches and flasks of tea – flasks of tea and sandwiches. God, am I fed up with bloody sandwiches. If I weren't so damn lazy I'd bring the gas stove more. How many variations can you make with cold meat, Pan

Yan bloody pickle and slices of bloody bread? Not a bloody lot, I can assure you. Sandwiches at work, too, on bloody nights. Now those hot bacon sandwiches Susan and I used to buy from the little snack bar near King's Cross station were sandwiches to mouth-water at.

* * *

By September 19th, the water temperature was becoming colder by the day. Not this year an Indian Summer. Arriving at the lake, I hopped out of my tired old car and went into the Moped in the hopes of seeing a carp. I saw several. To make my excuses beforehand, you understand, I should say that I did not really expect to hook a fish.

I fetched a rod and some bait from the car and crept down the sandy incline to the swim. After flicking in some Go Cat hoops, a fish of about fifteen pounds began taking bits off the surface in the open water to the right. When it went into the surface weed and started eating the hoops, I cast a small piece of hot-dog sausage near to it. The bait was soon taken out but the strike pulled the hook straight out of the carp's mouth and it scooted off.

Rain was falling, but the leafy boughs above me kept the worst of it off my clothes. By now carp were moving about and within five minutes three good fish were under the weed, eating the Go Cat. Extending the rod, I swung out a single hoop, landing it on the weed, near to a fish. The bait promptly floated off the hook and was soundly cursed. The next bait was a piece of sausage which I kept my eye on as the rain, blown in my face by the freshening breeze, came down even harder.

I was convinced the carp would go away in the face of this fresh onslaught by Mother Nature, but no, they seemed oblivious to the rain and kept right on sucking in the cat food. Through the weed I could see a fish's mouth working, just under my bait, and tensed in expectation.. The bait sunk into the maw of the carp and he was on. He boiled on the surface, sending waves rippling through the hornwort, but the weed, being very soft, was nothing to worry about with a tight line to break it and the fish near the surface. The fish didn't want to fight very hard, anyway, and was soon within range of the net. The trouble was I had not expected to hook a fish so I had left my net in the car.

I had to let the fish swim around for a while as I knew I would need to tire it before trying to pick it up. When it was close to the bank the outcome

Smashing!

of the fight seemed more dubious than ever, because I could see the hook was just stuck in a tiny flap of skin on the upper lip. Eventually, I judged him to be ready to land and stood in the water, drawing the fish gently to me. Crouching down and praying the tenuous hook-hold would not let me down. One violent move on the part of the fish would have been enough to end the fight with me in metaphorical tears. Everything held, though, and as the fish edged nearer I put an arm round him, dropped the rod, clasped the fish to my chest and walked up the bank. Wet and slimy I was, but the weight of the fish, at 17lb 12oz helped me brush aside my discomfort. Smashing!

The night in the Hidey Hole was spent with the expectation of a large fish as they are often seen in this area – I landed a torpedo common of 9lb 4oz! Of course, having to work in the day I was putting in some sleep, relying on the buzzers to wake me. Several butt-ringing bites occurred but I was wakened too late to hit them. It is a pity I didn't stick to fishing only whilst I was capable of fishing properly.

The last three fish that summer came from the Hidey Hole; as well as the one already mentioned, I caught a common of 16lb 14oz and a 10lb 1oz leather, both on hot-dog sausage.

It had proved to be an interesting summer, although not the greatest of my life. A few things had, at least, been learned. Luckily, the bad patches had been interspersed with productive ones, but, as usual, it had been a pleasure to fish Mywater, no matter what the results.

* * *

CHAPTER 8

Like a Monkey up a Stick

Sitting in my cottage, with Ultra Vox, Bob Marley and John Cooper Clarke headphoning their way into my brain, I can take stock. I have had some strange years at the lake, with fish rarely coming at a nice, steady rate. I am not sure why the carp react as they do; perhaps there are enough clues in this book for the discerning reader to make some order of the chaos. If I knew I could go every day to Mywater and catch a double figure carp, then I doubt if it would hold my interest for long.

I do not fish Mywater as much now as in the past, partly because I live further from it now, and also because I have done just about all there is to do there. The lake is more of a change of scenery than a challenge now. I was going to say it is more for my relaxation, but, as the log for this final summer will show, I had a far from relaxing time, being on the move for much of the time I spent there. I think Mywater is a place for fidgets and I am the type to fidget. Only time will tell how many more days I spend on the banks of Mywater. With other waters coming on and nearer to hand, I suppose my time will be restricted.

I did no close season work at Mywater in the form of baiting up or fish spotting. I knew that hot-dog sausage was going to work well, so I had a good bait to start off with.

Up until June 26th I fished another water. On my first visit to Mywater, by necessity a short one because Susan was with me and the kids were soon due in bed, I landed two fish – 9½lb and 13½lb. Both were caught on the top on hot-dog sausage, floating with the help of a tablet of floater at each end of the bait. The floater had been rolled ¼" thick, baked, then stamped into 'tablets' with a length of steel tubing sharpened round the rim. Self-raising flour and water were the main constituents with a suitable smell added, in this case curry powder. I do not think the crust made any difference to the bait – they were just happy to grab a free helping of sausage. Not so free, though. I myself was happy to have caught something for my long suffering wife. She is also as pleased with what I land as I – sometimes more, funnily enough.

Saturday 28th June was dull, with a south wind blowing as I parked my car and went down to the water for a look round. Surprisingly, there were no anglers on the bank, perhaps because little had been caught since the season had begun. I climbed up the spotting tree by the Moped Swim and saw several carp there, including a common, near to twenty pounds. As the fish were moving through the reeds into the Special I decided to set up there.

Tackling up three rods, I put hot-dog sausage bits on them all. One was cast to the surface dead reeds to the left where they had accumulated. The second I cast just short of these reeds, the bait sinking into six feet of water. I put a float on the third rod and fished that bait on the bottom next to the sunken tree, scene of so many agonising moments over the years.

Sitting on the planks of wood Oz and I had put against the back of the swim to help shore up the sloping, crumbling bank, I watched as odd fish swam across my line of vision.

After I had been waiting for one and a half hours – the time was 3.45 p.m. – I decided to give it until 4.00 p.m., before moving swims. My eyes roamed from the watch face to the water, and saw a very big fish swim past the sunken tree, from the right, and slowly sink downwards. I stood up and moved to the water's edge, peering over the cover to see the fish, tail up and heading down, out of sight into seven feet of murky water.

Not, I must admit, expecting a take from such a big fish, I nonetheless reeled in the float gear to where I thought the fish was, and released the bale arm, watching the 1" long lump of sausage sink gracefully into the twilight. The float lay flat on the surface as it was by now over depth, but I ignored that and watched the line. Half a minute was all I had to wait before the line began to slide through the float's eye. I reeled in the slack line and struck into a big 'un.

Obviously being in an optimistic mood that day, I had left on the Jack Hilton the ten pounds nylon line I had been using at the previous water and instantly regretted not having my terylene on. As the carp plunged deep down into the water, it was too late for regrets. It was a hard, exhilarating fight, with 'grass' rising to the top in patches and silt clouds blooming up in the water like a series of slow-motion explosions, but the fish did not try too hard to reach the tree, so I was happy enough as there is no tough weed to contend with in this area.

After five minutes or so, the jogging of the rod lessened and I began to think that as long as the hook held I would be okay, and so it was, with the swim devastated on the bottom by the carp's struggles. I broke my landing net pole in half, for the millionth time, before grasping what was left and slipping the net into the water to encompass the fish.

That one weighed 26lb 6oz., just beating my long-time personal best (14 years) of 26lb.

I was over the moon. After the photographs had been taken, I slipped the carp back into the water in the Moped and went for a walk round. The pictures, as has often been the case with me, failed to come out.

I have never caught two twenties in a day from Mywater. Two in a season is good fishing, but sometimes conditions are right for bigger than average fish and some good ones were moving that day. Unfortunately, I lost the next fish I hooked.

Using a twig as a float, I fished the Secret Place and some five hours after the big fish, I struck as the 'float' lay flat. The carp crashed on the top, somehow got through some snags and the terylene broke. I had had a good look at that fish and the second look, when he leapt out of the water, confirmed my earlier estimate of the size; it was as near to twenty pounds as dammit. In the space of a few hours it is possible to scale the heights then sink to the depths; I finished fishing after losing that carp, big ones about or not.

Next day I went to Mywater again, this time with Jay as a companion. Nige and Kev were there, the latter arriving at the same time as I and electing to fish Elliott's Swim. Nige had been in No.1 since eleven.

I put my gear in the Special, but wandered about looking for fish until, a couple of hours after arriving, I spotted something moving in the suicide spot. My swan shot/float tackle was soon bedded down and a few minutes only passed before I had a take which I missed. A short while later, the float again went flat and I was into a fish which did not fight very well – considering the position it was in I suspect it was scared of being sliced to death. The biggest difficulty was getting my net into the water through the reeds, but I managed that task, despite a few palpitations and a fat, $15^1/_2$lb leather was safe and sound.

Some fish were swimming in the Moped Swim, so I cast a sausage bait, float fished, to the far bank, where it tangled itself with a bush. A spot of pulling and persuasion cleared the bait which plopped nicely into the water, but the float wouldn't cock. It was some seconds before I realised the bait had been taken 'on the drop'; so quick a take was a bit like chub fishing and the fish was about the right size for chubbing too, at 5lb!

I saw six carp in the New Swim, my next port of call, four of them pushing the twenty mark. I quickly set up my rods. One sausage was cast to the right, alongside the bank, the other two rods, baited with baked beans and sausage (different bait on each rod), were float-fished and the baits were dropped on the clear, raised strip of clay in front of the opening. When the carp had hidden themselves again, I threw in a couple of handfuls of baked beans round the hook so baited.

After a while, I became bored so I went back through the Special, up the sandy bank to the lane at the back of the New Swim. As I watched, a carp swam towards the floats and began to sink to the bottom. I shot back the way I had come, taking the last few yards to my rods with a bit more care. Nothing happened.

Once more Polaroids as ever, perched on my nose, I went up the bank again to take up my former position. It was not long before a carp which I estimated at being near to twenty pounds, was going down to the baits, so I once again scurried to my rods. The bean bait was the nearest one the carp had been to when I had shifted station but, after a couple of minutes, the float on the hot-dog sausage slid under and I struck. A few feet of line was pulled off the clutch in the initial burst of power – then the hook pulled out. I was slightly cheesed off. After this upset I settled in the Special where I lost another fish through the hook pulling out. A hook as sharp as a razor, I might add.

During the next two days, two more fish were lost; seemingly I was back in another of those inexplicable periods where everything goes wrong, but I put a stop to the slide with a 15lb 12oz mirror from the top of the big willow (I was at the top of the tree, not the carp).

The wind on that day was blowing into No. 1 Swim and the carp were much in evidence there, the sun warming their backs. The hornwort was growing in a profusion that threatened to make bottom fishing impossible; on the credit side, the weed spread out on the surface in a mat which the carp were very happy to feed in. Top baits were taken frequently by the carp; and also by the roach which had acquired a taste for the cat food, attacking it with carp-sized smacks of the lips.

I caught a second double that day, fishing from the top of the tree. A fish just under 14lb came to the net after being selected from amongst several others as being the one which should be allowed a bite at my loaded bait. I had thought the carp somewhat larger. Methinks it was full of hydrogen. For five minutes I had 'played' that fish with the line running through the branches of a half sunken bush which just happens to lurk by the water against the reeds, between the tree and the Twenty Swim. All the fish needed was to move just once towards the open water and free the line but it took five minutes of sweating and cursing before it had the decency to do the honourable thing. The bait had been a couple of curry tablets, a bait the Mywater carp were very keen on.

The Author fishing Elliott's swim.

...He climbs the big willow like a monkey up a stick, that carp-man with eyes for nothing else. He boils, bakes, fries concoctions the like of which the carp have never seen, nor which they would want to see, given the choice. He scratches his face on the briers, curses the sweaty, itchy armpits, picks a dusty nose, tears fingernails on knots round hooks – knots which, once tied, will not be untied, but have to be sliced to death with a razor blade. He listens to his music on the car radio; sings his head off to the latest hits, the thrill of pleasure at the instruments and voices coursing down his spine. He listens, too, when no one is about, to the transistor emitting its music through the air. He listens, again, to the Test Matches between the former penal colony called Australia, where his father was born, and England, willing his heroes to thrash the Aussies into the dust – those lager-drinking, golden skinned Sheila lovers. He reads and reads the endless supply of science-fiction books whilst eating Pot Noodles, or honey-coated slices of bread, or guiltily smoking cigars. He chats with the fisherman who are trying their luck; a laugh here, a joke there, but all the time the brain is working on the method and way to catch the carp. Why doesn't he try something different? He could be a good tench fisher, a fine bream basher. Why doesn't he go for a species other than smelly old carp in the summer? Ask the him we are talking about....

* * *

The lake saw nothing of me during the rest of July, nor did I fish much in August, being caught up in a campaign on another water which demanded my full attention. Mywater produced some fish, but nothing of note. Four twenties had been landed in the first two weeks, including my own, but none since.

When the year had progressed into the last week of August I needed to relax a little, so a visit to Mywater might have been on the list of doctor's orders. The first fish I caught was a common, an ounce under sixteen pounds, from the Secret Place, an area I had fished but rarely on my previous trips this season, despite putting in quite an amount of bait. I was still hoping to see a really big one in there before mucking up the swim again. In any case, I had officially banned the rest of the syndicate members from going into the swim, so it hardly seemed fair that I should sit in it, upsetting those poor old carp anglers. From the signs on the deck it was obvious that more than my dainty footsteps had stirred the bank, so that possibly explained why the carp now frequented the swim less.

Some days after catching the common, I arrived at the water at 5.00 p.m. with Jay. Nigel, on the point of packing up, had had two carp during the day, both weighing $13^3/_4$lb. He had been having a good season with the local carp and by the end of the season had broken my doubles record on Mywater, by catching over twenty fish above ten pounds.

I set up in the Middle Swim and at dusk had a reel-spinner which fell off before I could strike home the hook. The rest of the night passed quickly, sleepily and fishless. After dawn, Jay tackled up in Elliott's Swim for his sprat catching and I spent the morning mooching along the north side in an attempt to coax a carp on to a hook. It wasn't until shortly after noon that some carp decided to feed, but cagily, on the Go Cat hoops I had catapulted into the New Swim.

Years ago, I discovered that fishing a different bait amongst a particle carpet picked up fish whilst the rod baited with the same type as the groundbait often failed. The next deduction was that the same criterion can be applied to surface feeding carp; if the fish are feeding cautiously on one particular food item – in this case the hoops – then a different bait might be taken. The use of the hot-dog sausage pieces on the surface amongst the hoops might not now seem so daft, but I think the carp view with some suspicion a bait which is floating, yet which is normally to be found on the bottom. This was especially true of hot-dogs on the surface near the big willow, yet on top of the surface weeds or broken reeds they are eaten confidently.

I had some of Jay's maggots with me, so I stuffed a dozen or so onto the hook and whipped the air to a cream in an attempt to cast the bait out far enough. The maggots dropped gently on the weed in the New Swim, the fish seemingly unaware of the small disturbance.

As they moved around, the carp neared the maggots, then one slowly passed close to my bait, spotted it, swam backwards a few inches and hit with its nose the weed the bait lay on. I do not know why that action was performed, but the next move by the fish was the one I had been hoping for – it sucked in the bait. And I struck.

The New Swim suffered a much-needed weed clearing job as the fish sought to break the ten pounds line, but I held on grimly and after a few minutes the net did its job and the carp was hauled from the water. 19lb 2oz of mirror. Yippee! The fish was put in a sack and tethered in the Special Swim, then I went to the west end and clambered up the willow. Sitting in the crook of the bough, the bait bag hanging on a nail I had knocked in the wood the year before, the rod resting between two branches, I flicked and catapulted hoops over a large area of No. 1 Swim. As I had expected, carp soon made their presence known and I spotted several decent fish, the biggest, near to the entrance of the Twenty Swim, cruising in a small area with a diminutive mirror as a companion. Neither fish was showing any interest in the surface bait. As I had no other floaters with me up the tree but the hoops, I was resigned to using them, so I put three rings on the hook, broke up a fourth (all from my 'damp' bag) and pushed a piece of it on the point of the hook to hold on the other three. The carp being in clear water, I did something I very rarely do; I cast the bait into the open water near to the fish as it swam with its back to me. This action was totally against all I have learned, over the years, but I tried it anyway.

The larger carp still hadn't taken bait as he turned and slowly swam against the reeds alongside the willow but he moved out, towards the patch of loose hoops my bait was amongst. Straight to my bait he went, ignoring the other feed, and stopped two inches from the line, the hook about three inches from his snout. I was convinced the line was being inspected and the carp would slip away, shortly, chuckling to himself at my naivete, but no!, he turned the few inches to his right and sucked in the bait. And with a score of free offerings all around it!

One hoop came free as the carp swirled and I thought that would be the one left with the hook in, but the line began tightening up, happily, and the strike resulted in a hooked fish. As the old merry-go-round began once more, I shouted to Jay to lend a hand, putting my finger on the reel clutch as the fish made for the reeds to my left, then tried to dig its way into the tree's fibrous roots. I pulled the carp away from the tree, allowing it to cause G.B.H. to the hornwort. That did the trick; with a mass of weed over its face it thought it was safe and gave up the fight. Jay was by now breathless from his run, but ready with the net below me. I towed the fish under the slanted trunk of that old willow tree and into the net. Dropping the rod into some soft weed, I slid down the trunk and lifted the net from the water.

The scales were back round the Middle Swim so I carried carp and net there, and hoisted my prize, the sweat prickling my forehead. 22lb exactly. I felt great! I sacked that one in Elliott's Swim, intending to take some photographs of both carp together.

For a reason which escapes me, I had to leave the water for a short time and on returning, Gary, who had arrived earlier, informed me that the larger fish had escaped through a hole in the sack, so I didn't get my photographs after all. I released the first-caught fish there and then.

During the night I slept well and was not interfered with by carp, nor much else, for that matter. During the subsequent day, I managed just one more fish, again from the willow, this time on hot-dog sausage cast on the the hornwort. At $10^1/_4$lb the fish was no monster, but I had had my share for the session, I thought.

During that day, whilst wandering around, Jay with me instead of catching his sprats, I came a nasty cropper. We had stood on the horizontal part of the willow's trunk for a while, looking at a carp near to our feet, when I decided to climb. I was six feet up when a foot slipped and I fell, landing with legs apart on a thick stub of branch jutting over the water. A tremendous pain in my back suggested I had broken it, whilst one in my backside indicated that a certain sensitive area had been ripped. As my feet dangled in the water, my panic subsided with the pain and I realised that I had not, in fact, injured myself seriously. I was very lucky, but it was inevitable that one day, tree-climbing, I would come a cropper. Funnily enough, I had been suffering from a bad back but that accident cured it. I would not suggest it as a regular cure for back-sufferers though.

During my downward flight, a pair of very expensive Polaroids had flung themselves off my nose and into the briny. I could not fish them out with net, or rod, or broken branches, so yet again I had to strip off and totally immerse myself in the chilly depths; luckily I held the glasses first duck.

This account of my years at Mywater is coming to a close as summer ended. I will finish by recounting the few days' fishing that brings my adventures up to date. Particularly, the last fish caught in the seven year period is the reason which finally prompted me to put in the work necessary to produce this book.

* * *

CHAPTER 9

Curtains for the Last Act

On the first Tuesday in September, I was at the water for 5.00 p.m., having driven straight from work. The weather during the previous days had been warm and kind, instilling in me a confidence that I could well catch some fish. A few carp were drifting about along the north side, so I catapulted in some Go Cat hoops, hoping to attract carp to the surface where I might be able to select a decent fish. As usual, I wandered about a lot, moving from swim to swim; little, though, was interested in a bait.

Time passed swiftly enough and I wondered whether I could hook a fish before dusk. On quietly skidding down the crumbly bank, I saw a big fish in the Little Tree Swim – for the first time that year.

With the usual gear of Micron, Jack Hilton rod and a black, thick wire salmon hook, I edged a little closer and poked the rod through the foliage. On the hook were half a dozen caterpillars which my children had found in my garden the day before. As the carp moved along the channel, I dangled the bait on the surface; the carp passed by and joined forces with several more of its species. When the carp were near the bait, only one, weighing perhaps twelve pounds, tried to suck in the meal. Both times he tried to eat it I pulled the bait off the surface, not wanting to hook that particular fish. After 45 minutes I saw two big carp lying to the left, near to the Swamp. I swung the caterpillars to my hand and moved a few feet, once again poking the rod through a gap in the bushes I had fortuitously made a week earlier.

The larger fish was now on the surface, so I dapped the caterpillars, seeing them wriggling enticingly; Mr. Carp ignored them completely! I then decided to let the bait sink. As the caterpillars were slowly lowered to the bottom, the carp showed obvious interest and began moving towards them. Before the mud was reached, however, the line tangled in the branches of the bush and I swore, but the carp, although slowing down, still moved in the right direction. Giving a mental shrug of the shoulders, I went for broke and raised the bait gently until it and the carp met in the middle. His bulk now hid the bait but I considered things to be in the right position and as the gill covers moved I struck, hooking the fish. In that sorely confined space the carp went mad, all twenty odd pounds of him, but I managed to hold on for, perhaps, fifteen seconds before he got under a bush to my right and grated the line. A few more seconds then the terylene broke and the rod flew back at me. I threw down the fibre-glass stick and walked away in disgust.

Later on, having calmed down, I took a rod up the big tree and saw two or three carp feeding on the hoops I had thrown in earlier. The biggest fish was soon directly below me and I lowered a bait to the water a little way from him. The bait was approached and the carp blew water, causing the bait to swirl, then he shot off, as if stung. A short while later the same fish came back, sucked in one or two free offerings, then the hook bait. I struck – and the hook came whizzing into the tree. I waited another half hour but it eventually became too dark to see what was happening below. The following evening found me again sitting up the tree.

The carp, after some time spent eyeing the loose hoops I had fed in, began, tentatively, to accept them. Baiting up my rod I held it below my feet and swung the hot-dog sausage lump in ever widening arcs until letting go of the line to allow the bait to plop on to the rubbish which the wind had pushed into the Twenty Swim corner. Pulling the bait back to surface level, I juggled the line into the right position, then saw a nice fish had appeared under the raft.

I watched keenly as a shape moved under the sausage – and the sausage was gone. That fish weighed 15lb. 9oz. and gave a good account of itself before I slid down the tree and netted it.

Loaded with missed chances a further few trips reared their naughty heads at Mywater, but I hooked nothing. My fishing time was due to be restricted because I had to build an extension to my cottage before winter set in so I knew I would have to fish waters nearer home at the expense of Mywater. I fact, I caught only one more carp from Mywater that season. Here is the tale of that final fish:

September 16th and my old Cortina gasped to a halt parked off the gravel of the lane on the grass the goats kept short. After diving down the bank to look in the Swamp and the Little Tree Swim, I catapulted floaters along the north side, as I had been doing for weeks. The intention was to feed with hoops and use my home-baked curry tablets on the hook. The nettles still grew where they could find a bare patch of earth; in profusion the briars scattered their thorny arms to the far reaches of this bank and I knew that a growing season without the trespass of anglers would see the north side choked up again.

Reaching the Moped Swim, I climbed the tree and saw eight doubles swim into sight, joining the one already there. Unfortunately, none of the fish showed any interest in my baits so I picked up my bits and pieces, hoisted rod and net and made my way to the Secret Place, where, happily, a brace of carp were eating the floaters I had put in earlier.

Instead of my terylene line, I used the 10lb. bs. nylon I had been casting in the Moped and the first carp to take my bait got moving and the line broke at the reel.

Cussing, back through the hedge on to the lane, along and through the barred gate I walked, and down the avenue of thorns which often reach down and rip my hat off my head. Sharp left turn down a small incline and through more hawthorns, reaching No. 1 Swim, one I sadly neglect. I stood for a while looking at the undisturbed length of the lake before moving to my right and the Rectangle.

Two days previously I had discovered that it was possible to fish between the thick reeds in the water and the hawthorn and bramble bushes tight to the water's edge. It had entailed some pushing (and getting scratched) to move along, also scaring off any carp in the reeds. The next day I had stood, ankle deep in the water, for some time in my new spot but although a fish or two had been around, I had not hooked one. I had seen, from that short stay, that an eleven foot rod was too long in the confined space, so, on the fateful day in question, I was sporting a rod something less than ten feet in length and of 2lb. test curve – and me wellies!

A decent fish showed, just below the surface in front of the conventional position and heading towards the same area I was in, so all seemed well.

I edged slowly along the little route I had made, stopping just fifteen feet or so in, then stood quietly, flicking in hoops and curry tablets. Movement in the reeds to the right indicated a fish, so with four tablets on the hook, I gently lobbed the tackle in the right direction. Although I could not see the bait, I knew that four baits just floated the No. 1 hook. Shortly, the line tightened and I struck into what felt like a good fish which moved only fractionally before the line broke with a loud crack. Even the Micron was doing it now. I was really peeved about that, thinking my lot was up for the day, and decided to pack up and go to the local tackle shop for some **thirty** pound test terylene. Before I could put my resolution into effect, the carp were at it again, clooping the baits in their reedy sanctuary. I hurriedly tied on another hook and baited it up.

A yard or so from my left foot a mouth was taking baits from the side of a clump of weed and I lowered the baited hook almost into its maw. The fish gulped and I struck, but the hook flew into the bushes behind me. I flicked in a half dozen more baits before extricating the hook from the foliage and considered that the carp, when it had bolted, had shown itself to be only a

small member of its species.

Still the carp clooped down the baits, obviously feeling very safe, surrounded by reeds, and a hook lowered to my right was quickly engulfed by a pair of rubbery lips. Again I struck and yet again, somehow, the bare hook came out of the mouth of a startled fish. Tosh!

I threaded on four more tablets and cast them further to the right, but still only two or three yards away, where fish could still be heard feeding off the surface. The thorns poked away at the back of my neck.

I could not see the bait this time, so I held a loop of line twixt thumb and finger, waiting for it to be tugged from my grasp. When the line **was** yanked, I struck and the rod was pulled into its battle curve by a big fish which shot through the reeds, towards open water. It was not an occasion for allowing the fish to carry on, however, so I braked him and began my usual praying session, knowing those reeds were so sharp. I pumped the fish back a way, so then considered it couldn't be a big one, but it thrashed about somewhat as it drew closer and the reeds parted, like the curtains for the last act, to reveal a big mirror.

Curtains for the Last Act

By the time he had given up creating froth, I had seen the hook was lodged firmly in the mouth, but plenty of broken reeds lay between us and the line was caught, near the hook, on one of them. I had no alternative but to batter down the intervening reeds with the landing net and this caused the fish to leap about some more, although the line stayed firmly in the reed stem near to our friend's snout.

The net was eventually submerged and somehow pushed up to the offending reed, but I just **knew** that line was going to part when I stabbed at that reed to free the fish. But no! The pushing freed the line and the pulling on the rod brought the fish forward and over the net. He was mine, all mine.

My scales and sack were in the car so I covered fish and net with my jacket and ran along the gloomy alleyway of hawthorns to my motor.

The fish had to be weighed in the landing net. Panting, eager to know if I had beaten my best ever for the second time that season, it wasn't too easy to subtract the weight of the net from the total weight, but I managed it, eventually.

So the fish of my lifetime weighed 27lb. 3oz. The yippee of the year escaped my lips.

I didn't really need to catch anything more from Mywater that season, did I?

CHAPTER 10

Tidying Up

"Arrgh!" a voice inside me cried, when in answer to my, "Good afternoon – Symak," the telephoner announced himself as Tim Paisley of the publishers of this book. Fear isn't the word to describe the emotion I've felt at every communication with Tim since my manuscript was accepted for publication – trepidation is more the word, I suppose. "Something is going to go wrong and it won't hit the shops. I know it," has been the dread for several long, lingering months. But no, he wasn't planning to tell me Paisley-Wilde Publishing had gone into liquidation; nor that they had decided to stop publishing fishing stuff; or, on second thoughts, my work just wasn't up to scratch, so sorry, but can we have our advance back? No, Tim, having done his final proof-reading, felt that there was something missing from the narrative and, what's more, he could put his finger on it. "The carp in the book don't have names," he said. "There is no recognition of fish from chapter to chapter." Ah, but there was still a bit of mystery around in the seventies and every carp hadn't been caught eighty three times and was distantly related to Chris Yates. But if Tim's perception is on the mark, perhaps I have a duty to explain what we had in the water and talk about some of the fish. Here goes:

It is fair speculation that just about all of the carp in Mywater must have been caught during the seventies, although not all were landed more than once or twice in the period the book covers. As one example of the elusiveness of some Mywater carp, I can cite the case of the two twenty plus commons: I have fished Mywater for twenty three years at the last count and haven't caught either of 'em. (This could be taken as a reflection on my abilities, I know!).

The largest fish in my story gained a name during the eighties – the Black Fish. Blunt Nose and Fred were the only other two fish to actually be bestowed with names. Nigel Bryant christened Blunt Nose. I think I christened Fred. The Black Fish was black!

Some of the fish in my story are repeat captures, sure, but of the photographs suitable for publication it is obvious that there were quite a few different fish to go at. As regards numbers, Nige and I both agree there was something like thirty fish over ten pounds in the lake during the seventies, with a few twenties to near thirty pounds and the mysterious 31. Quite a few of these fish were commons – not the easiest fish to recognise as individuals. I could probably recognise four of 'em, apart from the twenties.

My 18.14 was a long, tough scrapper; a dark fish, lean as a bantam weight. One was a mid-double I caught a time or three which had uneven lobes on its tail – the upper one being smaller than the bottom. There is a picture of this fish in the book. Another common which reached upper doubles had only one eye. We would refer to this fish as, 'the common with a blind eye,' or some such. Nobody ever called him Nelson or Cyclops (or Keyhole Kate).

Blunty, bless him, Mywater's favourite common, had a face which looked like it had done several rounds with a heavy-weight boxing champion. Blunty was partly dope and partly incapacitated (de-sensitised mouth) but he gave loads of people pleasure and was loved, if that is not too strong a word, by myself, Gary Spencer my partner, Clive Tomlin our bailiff and good mate and a few others of syndicates past and present. Blunty is now buried with the Black Fish, my kids' cat Tommy and another double, behind my swim (Elliott's Swim) and there is a suitable grave marker to acknowledge the Black Fish and Blunty.

Fred, with considerably more scales on his flanks than the majority of the mirrors in Mywater was instantly recognisable, so tagging him with a handle made sense. Unfortunately, as you will have read, Fred didn't live long enough to achieve fame and notoriety after his initial identification.

There was a fish, which over the years has fluctuated between 19 and 20 pounds, with a growth wart on one of its gill covers but we never thought to call him Warty or Cromwell, or whatever, even though he graced more than one landing net. A recognisable fish though.

A mid-twenty mirror, a decent photograph of which I never obtained in the seventies was another nice fish in the water. Quite a lot of scales this fish had, as did a few pounds smaller nineteen/twenty who is peeking out from one of the photos in the book.

Yet another well-scaled mirror, a photo of which is in the book, was caught two or three times in the seventies by myself. This lovely fish, hovering around the eighteen mark is still around, and has now made it to a (fluctuating) twenty. This fish was one of the three fish landed on the minced fish baits.

True leathers are few and far between, but *almost* leathers abound and can be very difficult to identify correctly. There were some such in Mywater and I have no doubt they were caught now and then. Don't forget, though, that we just did not land large numbers of Mywater carp for two reasons: our ineptitude and heavy losses in those bleeding reeds! The Black Fish, before he became such, was a pretty friendly cove. I caught him more than once, as did Nige and one or two others. This fish never did make thirty pounds, but size isn't always the main interest in my carp fishing, I must admit.

During the period spanned by the book, I ran the syndicate (still do, of course, one million mosquito bites later). I kept the membership fairly small and for the most part, chose people who lived well out of the area so the place wouldn't be over-run by locals fishing every five minutes (I did not then, as I do now, have a 48 hours per week per member limit). As I didn't often see what the others caught and I hardly ever saw their photographs, the mystery of the fish in Mywater remained. Nowadays, in Mywater as in all the others, photographs are rather a prerequisite of fishing, so they tend to get bandied about much more, hence the fish become familiar. Also, of course, we've got better at pulling 'em out, so not many have escaped scrutiny, this past ten years at least.

Before I mention the 31 and end this extra chapter, there are just a few more things I would like to say:

Having identified and talked of some of the Mywater carp, we are still left with quite a few individuals in the seventies, some over twenty pounds (Ginger's 28 for example) which came and went with a certain amount of anonymity. Rubbish photographs, inaccurate descriptions, lack of contact between syndicate members who came from the far-flung corners of the Empire to fish in my little pond, even secrecy, which we were all guilty of in those days, all conspired to draw a veil over the general picture. The origin of the Mywater carp, worthy of a chapter in itself, has not been discussed, but forms part of another story which, in the not too distant future, I will set down on paper. In a tale spanning over 35 years, what has happened at Mywater in the eighties, the Chronicle and my syndicate, all have their parts!

So the biggest Mywater carp (until the eighties) and probably the biggest Mywater mystery of all; Pete Hall's 31. There is no doubt about the fish's authenticity. Those in the know would never doubt Pete's integrity and his ability to catch fish. From Pete's own description, the 31 wasn't the Black Fish, it being of shorter, deeper proportions, never mind about the weight gap. I did see what I thought was this 30 around the time of its capture, but, of course, one can always speculate wrongly about the size of fish, so the evidence before my eyes was not, as it were, concrete. That such a fish was not caught (as far as we know) before, or hasn't been landed since Pete's remarkable capture, just adds a little more flavour to the mystery that is carp fishing. The less than romantic view, propounded by Nige, is that Pete's carp was a spawn-bound one and it went away and quietly died. But it had to be an upper twenty anyway, so by the standards of the water and the day, it was still a big fish.

* * *

Postscript

When I was a youngster, living in Scarborough, the word carp not then part of my vocabulary, I used to paddle in the fast-running waters of the local beck, two or more miles from my home. Underneath the myriad stones and boulders of the cold, shallow stream, lurked the bullheads and stone loach, small fish I would delight in chasing with my hands and placing in jam jars for transportation home to observe until the inevitable death through lack of oxygen. I did not know then, of course, why the fish died so quickly. That kind of childhood memory still remains, as crystal clear as the water I used to paddle in. Perhaps my chasing of carp in later years is because of a germ planted in my brain as a stone loach-catching boy.

I recall, too, climbing the steep-sided banks of the beck, sometimes tumbling, always becoming muddy, shoes scuffed, fingers painfully reminded of the sharpness of gorse. Perhaps I still think little of struggling up trees, risking serious accident, because, nearly thirty years ago, I found that climbing is much more fun than walking a flat footpath. I suppose that the day is drawing nearer when I will have to stop emulating the monkey – pity that day should come. Pity that I should even have to contemplate it.

I know that my enjoyment of fishing is likely to continue: I am in a mould now, after three decades' interest in things that swim with such grace and energy through the silver waters. Once my eyes looked at the beck and the vast sea it flowed into, by the side of which was my home; now it is the enclosed acreage of a clay or gravel lake which captures my interest.

There is so much to see – so much yet to discover about my fish. I have the rest of my life to enjoy the discoveries; the sight of a gleaming creature freshly plucked from its environment excites me dreadfully. And when I am old and grey, too old, indeed, to stand the strains of all that carp fishing entails, perhaps I will be fishing a clear, running stream for small fish – something like the bullheads and stone loach I used to catch by hand as a freckle-faced ragamuffin.

* * *